# HERALDS OF THE KING

# HERALDS OF THE KING

*By*

## THE REVEREND JOHN G. HOGAN

*Essay Index Reprint Series*

*originally published by*

THE STRATFORD COMPANY

 **BOOKS FOR LIBRARIES PRESS**
**FREEPORT, NEW YORK**

First Published 1934
Reprinted 1970

[1970, c1934]

STANDARD BOOK NUMBER:
8369-1516-X


LIBRARY OF CONGRESS CATALOG CARD NUMBER:
79-107714


PRINTED IN THE UNITED STATES OF AMERICA

INTERNATIONAL CHRISTIAN
GRADUATE UNIVERSITY

NIHIL OBSTAT,
     Patrick J. Waters, Ph.D.
       *Censor Librorum.*

IMPRIMATUR,
     † William Cardinal O'Connell,
       *Archbishop of Boston.*

## Author's Declaration

IN OBEDIENCE to the decrees of Pope Urban VIII we declare that in the pages relating to the Servant of God, Mother Elizabeth Ann Seton, we do not attempt to anticipate the judgment of the Church, but in all things we submit to the judgment of the Church.

**Dedicated**

TO THE

BLESSED VIRGIN MARY

GOD'S MOTHER AND OUR MOTHER

# Contents

# Preface

THE PURPOSE of this volume is to set before men
the ideals and principles that worked such a tremendous amount of good for mankind through
the lives of St. Francis of Assisi, St. Dominic, St.
Ignatius of Loyola, St. Teresa of Avila, St. Jane
Frances de Chantal, and Mother Elizabeth Ann
Seton.

Individuals, and society as a whole, disillusioned
by the false tenets that have prevailed, are ready
to accept a philosophy of life that will ensure
peace and happiness. These noble men and women,
by following certain definite ideas, were able to
attain to contentment of soul themselves, and to
furnish it to a host of others who came under their
guidance and influence. The same helpful and
powerful message which they enunciated to their
own times with such success for millions, they
expound still to those who are willing to listen to
the interesting story of their struggles and victories. Each one of them was able to win thousands to an organization for the bringing of their
teachings to the masses. St. Francis of Assisi alone
gave a new and glorious complexion to the world
in which he lived. The other characters portrayed

i

were a power for good to a greater or less degree.

It is confidently hoped that men and women seeking the fountain of truth and goodness may find it through these great Christian heroes. The time is ripe for the diffusion of the beneficent scheme of life they propagated. If this book awakens individuals in every walk of life to an appreciation of the necessity, of the value, and of the wisdom of seeking first the kingdom of God and His justice, it will have served the purpose of its composition.

THE AUTHOR.

*The Annunciation of the Blessed Virgin. 1934.*

# HERALDS OF THE KING

❦

## St. Francis of Assisi

IF IT BE true that "all the world loves a lover,"
then all mankind should be in love with St. Francis
of Assisi. This humble, mediæval saint of poverty
is the lover *par excellence*, the one most heroic and
most romantic. Here is a character that would do
credit to any modern novelist; here is verified
the adage that truth is stranger than fiction. The
thread that makes up this life of paradoxes, the
secret of the many, varied traits, is a mighty,
unbounded, unselfish passion. Unlike other love
stories, however, the friendship of Francis is not
for a creature but for the Creator. As men and
women learn to love the heroes of their books, so
all who follow the story of this strange genius of
the Middle Ages should find in their hearts a
great enduring devotion to the Poor Little Man
of Assisi.

The beginnings of the life of our Saint are not
what one expects to find. Francis was no poor
child who became marvelously rich; he was a rich
one who became uncommonly poor. His father,

dream in which he saw a room filled with the accoutrements of war, while a voice said, "All this shall belong to you and your warriors." A legend states that when he was fitted out in the finest panoply that money could buy, and on his way to battle, he had an attack of fever in Spoleto. As he lay there, more dead than alive, a voice asked him where he was going. "To Apulia, to be a knight," the proud youth replied. "Tell me, Francis, who can benefit you most, the Lord or His servant?" the voice asked. "The Lord," was the immediate response of Francis. "Then why do you desert the Lord for the servant, and the Prince for the vassal?" It was then that he realized that God was the Voice. "Lord, what do you wish me to do?" The Master answered, "Go back to your home; there it shall be told you what you are to do. For the vision you saw must be understood in another way."

This episode explains the change that came over our happy-go-lucky troubadour. Back went the much-decorated soldier to face the questionings of his disappointed friends, but also the will of God. Although he still enjoyed the excitements of youth, even his light-hearted companions noticed often a seriousness on the countenance that before was ever gay. Now his usual haunts no longer claimed him. Stealthily he has been obtaining refuge and

4

quiet in an abandoned cave near a ruined church just outside the city, gradually giving up altogether his former associates. He would pass long hours in meditation, seeking further light from the Savior. Only one friend enjoyed his confidence; together they would go to the mountain-retreat. Now he could say:

> "I walk a solitary way, apart
>   From friends who once were near and dear to me.
> For God demands an undivided heart,
>   And only lonely souls are wholly free."

Pietro was away on business and did not know this development. The attentive Madonna Pica observed the change, but like a prudent soul, asked no questions. Francis' face was pale and haggard from his vigils and fastings. He still gave feasts but now they were to the poor he met on his journeys. Between his visits to churches and his care of the beggars all his time was taken up.

About this time, perhaps in the year 1205, he made a pilgrimage to Rome to visit the tombs of the apostles. While there he did something which indicates his new spirit. Picture in beggar's rags at the door of one of the great Roman basilicas, the noble son of Assisi's richest merchant, the former proud, boisterous leader of the town's social set. As Christ put Himself in the place of man, Francis exchanged his fine clothes for the

rags of the beggar that he might at once humble
himself, and also realize the plight of the poor.
On his return to his home, he again spent most of
his days, like St. Benedict of Nursia, in his little
cave on the hillside. While making his way thither
one day alone, he was beset by brigands who
stripped him and demanded who he was. "I,"
dramatically replied Francis, "am the herald of
the Great King." The accuracy of this great characterization of his vocation will only be appreciated as one sees later Francis' power by word
and example of proclaiming his Master.

It was while engaged in prayer in the little hillside church at San Damiano that another dramatic
event occurred; one destined to bring on the crisis
in the career of our hero. The year was 1207. As
Francis, with his eyes uplifted to the crucifix,
begged Almighty God to make known to him his
life-work, a voice from the crucifix suddenly said,
"Now, go hence, Francis, and build up My house,
for it is nearly falling down." Always obedient,
Francis proceeded to carry out the injunction by
repairing the abandoned chapel. This work in-
volved him in more serious consequences than one
would expect. Funds were needed to buy the necessary stone. The same good-natured youth of old
took some of the rolls of cloth from the shop of
his father, loaded them upon a donkey, and set off

for the market. Along with the merchandise, Francis also sold the beast. The money obtained would not only be a means of building San Damiano, but the occasion for Francis to commence that vocation which would renew the universal church.

Francis' father now enters the picture, at first one thinks to spoil it. He had been away during the change in the conduct of his heir. Business was to Pietro a vital, engaging, consuming matter. Imagine the surprise, therefore, of him who had visioned noble deeds for his son, on looking out of the store to learn the cause of a commotion in the street, finding his Francis dressed in beggar's rags, and followed by a crowd of mocking boys. Pietro never wanted for a decision. This outrageous behavior would be speedily settled. Such fool conduct for whatever reason, would come to a quick conclusion. Francis was arrested for the theft of the rolls of cloth. Not excited by this step, the culprit declared that, as a subject of the Church, he had to be tried in its court. Evidently he was tonsured. As Festus said to Paul, "Hast thou appealed to Cæsar? To Cæsar shalt thou go," so Pietro was ready for all emergencies; before the bishop he would lead this unruly son for correction.

The scene that followed was a most dramatic

one. The case itself offered no problem. The bishop, while he had given counsel to Francis in his prayers and charity, had to judge that the cloth and consequently the money obtained, belonged to the father. Francis was ready for the settlement. "My Lord," he said to the bishop, "I will not only give him the money cheerfully, but the clothes I have received from him." Like a rapid change artist, the youth stepped into an ante-room; reappeared in his clothes of rags; and placed at the feet of the enraged parent the fine raiments which he had put on for the court scene. Then he triumphantly exclaimed, "Hitherto I have called Pietro Di Bernadone father. Now I return to him his money and all the clothes I obtained from him so that hereafter I shall not say, 'Father Pietro Di Bernadone, but Our Father Who art in heaven.' "

This was the end of that act in the drama of Francis' life, as he had announced. In the next appearance he is the servant and follower of Christ. One cannot help reflecting on the changed status of the child of Pietro and Madonna Pica. Born in luxury, he enjoyed its advantages and accepted its pleasures, until the Voice of God called him to serve Him. Once he saw the Will of the Master, unlike the rich young man in the gospel, this product of the Middle Ages did not

# ST. FRANCIS OF ASSISI

hesitate in his allegiance. To be of service to his Savior, to minister to the poor and neglected, Francis the son of wealth, became the poorest of men. He did not stop to declare that he had great possessions. Leaving behind him his father's house with its comforts and luxuries; renouncing the inheritance that would guarantee him ease and self-indulgence; he put on the raiments of the poor, and sought for a home,—the cave on the mountain side. Like the Son of Man, henceforth, he "had not whereon to lay his head." He was seen on the streets of his beloved Assisi, having for raiment, the grey woolen cloak of a peasant, the hood covering his head, a piece of rope tied about his waist. His greeting was to all, "The Lord give you peace," and if there were many at hand, he would follow this with a little sermon on the love of God for men. The completeness of this dedication, the generosity of it, makes us realize how very little we are willing to do for God. We, perhaps, are more like the rich young man in the gospel. The sacrifice of Francis should awaken in all Christian hearts a determination to imbibe something of his spirit and should prompt many souls to follow more closely in the footsteps of the Master.

Three episodes that came in this period of our hero's career have a right to be mentioned. There

9

was the meeting with his father on the roadside.
The bitter wrath and disappointment had not lost
any of its force. Francis saw the figure in the distance and his impulse was to avoid it. After all, he
said to himself, he had done the heroic act; why
involve himself in further humiliation? Perhaps
the father had already in his strong determination
to break this stubborn son, planned some new
measure to cower his offspring. The more Francis
thought, the greater became the desire to avoid
the encounter. It was enough to accept the rebuke
of strangers; it was not necessary to expose himself to his father anew. As he began to retreat, his
true spirit reproached him; was he ashamed of the
course he had taken? Was he to deny the Master
Whose livery he bore? The grace of God asserted
itself. He continued his steps; he received meekly
the wrath, even the curse of the angry father for
the greater glory of God. As he walked down the
hill he found himself with a greater peace than
ever before, the joy that God promised to those
who leave father and mother for the kingdom of
God.

The second incident was more repulsive; it
touched his natural feelings, his long-cherished
self-love. He had always possessed sympathy for
the unfortunate lepers; he had never, however,
been able to endure them. An offering would be

hurled from a distance as Francis ran off in haste. One day after his change of heart while Francis was riding alone, reflecting on the message God had spoken to him, a leper cried out to him. The old spirit manifested itself; the impulse was to make a hasty retreat. At the same time, the new Francis came to the surface. If he were in earnest in his petitions to serve his Master, here was an opportunity. Christ had said, "Inasmuch as you did it to one of these, my least brethren, you did it to Me." Fearful lest his resolution should waver, he jumped from the horse, gave the leper an offering, and at the same moment embraced the unfortunate man. The grace of the Savior had done its work; the lover of God was also a lover of God's afflicted. Self, that arch-enemy of all advanced religious fervor, had been dealt a telling blow.

A greater test was, however, awaiting the neophyte. It came as he was employed in begging from door to door for the church at San Damiano. Before he realized it he happened upon the house where his former jolly companions were enjoying their festivities. A dread came upon him such as he never before underwent. What a subject for ridicule he would now be! What jokes would be hurled at him by these frivolous celebrators! Worldly wisdom dictated a departure to other houses. Let well enough alone. He was in God's service, but as Robert Burns has said, "A man's a man for a' that." No good would come from a visitation here. The soul of him who had put on the beggar's rags in Rome spoke. He was doing the work of God. Let him take the humiliation that came with it. Let him not be ashamed of the gospel, or be too proud to acknowledge that he was a follower of the Man of Poverty. Into the gathering he went asking of all offerings for the beauty of God's house. This victory over his pride was the avenue to many precious graces. The son of Pietro was now in truth the servant of Jesus Christ. The grain of wheat that had fallen into the ground and died, would now bring forth much fruit. He that had lost his life had also found it. These three battles and victories were the key to future greatness. Francis had won where many others had fallen in defeat. Self-conquest is the most desirable of all prizes. Men who can rule and sway others, are unfortunately often unable to dominate their own inclinations. The seed that had been planted was now strong and hardy; it had borne with the early frosts; it would give to the Church of God an abundant harvest. "He that ruleth his own spirit is greater than he that taketh walled cities."

Untrammelled by home ties, unshackled from

self-love, the troubadour of Assisi now let loose his energies in the cause of the Lover to Whom he had given his heart. Like a real spouse he would stop at no contradiction to prove his sincerity. He continued his zeal for the renovation of churches, the earthly abodes of God. It was while thus daily engaged that others began to admire his humility, his sincerity, his self-effacement, his kindness to the poor. Having restored the Benedictine church of St. Peter, he worked on a little chapel called Portiuncula, that is, "a little portion of the earth," which was destined to become the home of a most marvelous religious order, formed by our Saint. Francis never gave up this early passion for the glory and beauty of God's house. He passed it on to his disciples and followers, both men and women. It was one of the most prominent characteristics in his make-up. He would never tolerate an abode of Almighty God being neglected. This spirit of reverence, of respect, of zeal for the neatness and sacredness of the Church should pulse through every sincere Christian. Any one who has faith in the Blessed Sacrament, in the tremendous mystery of the Holy Sacrifice of the Mass, must always be conscious of the reverence due to the Church, and possess a living passion for its comeliness and beauty. Not without reason does the Church keep before her children the verse of the royal psalmist, "I have loved, O Lord, the beauty of Thy house, and the place where Thy glory dwelleth."

The quiet example of our Saint was exercising an influence on others. Goldsmith, telling of the village preacher, says:

> "Truth from his lips prevailed with double sway,
> And fools who came to scoff, remained to pray."

The persevering devotion of this son of the rich merchant of the town, awoke the consciences of others. Verily "his strength was as the strength of ten, because his heart was pure." Men saw the value of his work for God, of his assistance to the lepers and the beggars. His first convert, like some of Our Lord's early followers, did not leave his name to posterity. Then came a rich tradesman, Bernard, who having sold all his goods for the poor, imitated the poverty and charity of his guide. The numbers now grew apace. There is the story told of Francis going with some of his followers to the book of gospels for advice, and opening to the passage, "If thou wilt be perfect, go sell what thou hast, and give to the poor, and follow Me." For this there was need of no establishment. The life was truly apostolic; they lived it together, begging their modicum of food, ministering to the sick and needy.

# ST. FRANCIS OF ASSISI

The time did come, however, when because of the increase of numbers, it was necessary to have some governing rule. This, like their life, was most simple. It provided for their poverty chiefly, their preaching in the streets and squares, their work among the sick, their prayers in common, first at Portiuncula, then at Rivo Torto. It was while at this latter place that our Saint decided to go to Rome to gain approval from the Pope for his order. According to tradition, the little band made the journey together to the imperial city. Whenever, while traveling, they came to a church or saw a cross in the distance, they would all bow down to the ground and say, "We adore Thee, O Christ, here, and in all Thy churches over the whole world, and we bless Thee because by Thy Holy Cross Thou has redeemed us." At the See of Peter, Francis met a friend, Bishop Guido of Assisi. The latter introduced him to one of the cardinals, who, when satisfied with his sincerity and practicality, acquainted the Holy Father, Innocent III, with the desires of our Saint. The Pope feared the severity of the mode of life portrayed. Many of the older cardinals discouraged the idea. Cardinal John, advocate for the friars, then spoke up, "These men only want us to allow them to live after the gospel. If we now declare this is impossible, then we declare the gospel can

not be followed, and thus insult Christ Who is the
origin of the gospel." These words carried the
day for the cause. Francis was soon summoned to
the Holy Father and received the approbation so
ardently desired. In 1210, therefore, The Friars
Minor, with Francis as head, became an auxiliary
order of the Church with permission to preach the
gospel.

With renewed enthusiasm the good brothers
preached the Word of God as they traced their
way back from Rome to Assisi. As they journeyed
they sang the praises of God, using at times the
beautiful poems that Francis composed. All the
cities through which they passed obtained the blessings that emanated from these devoted servants
of holy poverty. The people, captivated by their
example and preaching, each one of whom was
another Francis, were moved to penance and new
love for their religion. Their journey was like a
mighty forest fire, consuming all in its path. Not
only did they awaken the faith of the populace so
that their daily lives were more in accord with the
mind of Christ, but they won many men to their
company. The order was growing a hundredfold.
The whirlwind had now started. Its effect would
be felt for centuries to come. Now in very truth
the house of the Lord that was falling down and
going to ruin, would be renewed and embellished.

# ST. FRANCIS OF ASSISI

That glorious work, given by the Master to the son of Pietro Di Bernadone, was now being accomplished. The greatness of our Saint will be revealed in the marvelous spiritual conquests of his preachers throughout all Europe.

Along with this zealous interest in the upbuilding of the Church of God, Francis manifested a wonderful devotion to the lesser creation. His love for nature, for the flowers of the field, the birds of the air, even the animals of the forest, as well as inanimate creation beggars narration. He regarded each as a member of the Kingdom of the Heavenly King. All were so many sermons proclaiming the power and goodness of His Lover. The excellent poems he composed in praise of Brother-Sun, Sister-Moon, Mother-Earth, survive even to this day. He had a particular devotion to the lowliest and simplest because in them he saw the handiwork of his Lord. Many fanciful, if legendary stories, tell of his talking with the birds and taming wild beasts. What is evident from these accounts is that the creature was forever heralding to Francis his Creator, and that his love for the Creator prompted him to be devoted to His creatures.

It was at this stage that a young girl of Assisi, named Clare, accompanied by a female relative, made a secret visit to Francis. She was a comely maiden, from a very wealthy and socially prominent family. With her three sisters and her brother, she enjoyed all the advantages that money and influence could obtain. She, however, had not sought after social prestige. Always prayerful, she had been early attracted by the strong, sincere preaching of Francis in the cathedral church of the town. To him now she came for advice regarding her future. Three years before, when she was fifteen years old, a suitor sought her in marriage. Clare had quickly rejected the offer. Rebuked by her mother, she told her that she wanted only to serve God, and had consecrated her heart to Him alone. It seems evident that at that time Francis had been consulted, had approved her course and had urged perseverance. The purpose of the visit now was to ask permission to leave her home to fulfill the desires of her soul. Francis acquiesced in her ideas, and with her relative made plans for the consecration of this devoted virgin, now eighteen years old, to the service of Him, "to serve Whom is to reign." On Palm Sunday evening, Clare eagerly left her father's rich and comfortable home, accompanied by the same relative, went to Portiuncula where she renounced the world, dedicated herself to God, and then temporarily entered a convent of the Benedictine Sisters.

# ST. FRANCIS OF ASSISI

All the entreaties and threats of the angry father were without fruit. Clare, deeply in love with God, had made a serious step only after much prayer and long deliberation. Her will was firm by the grace of God. The efforts of the paid emissaries of the distraught parent availed nothing. To his dismay, a younger sister, Agnes, joined Clare. This was the beginning of a glorious institution for the cause of Christ. When others desired to live the same life of prayer and self-effacement, Francis obtained the Church of San Damiano which he had, in his early fervor, repaired. There he established the first convent of the order known today as the Poor Clares. It was not long before this work, begun so humbly and simply, spread throughout Italy. In 1215 the order with Clare as head was approved by the Pope. Many devoted souls were anxious for such an opportunity to renounce the pleasures of the world, to consecrate themselves to a life of prayer and sacrifice for the good of souls in the world. The Sisters observed the rule of cloister, being supported by handiwork and the gifts brought by some of the friars. The order of women was always greatly attached to its spiritual father, Francis. Clare especially had a filial devotion to him, and followed in her own life his extraordinary example of poverty and mortification. In her spiritual daughters of today are found the same lofty ideals that were so earnestly sought by herself, which led the Church to proclaim this faithful follower a saint.

Francis now felt that having set in order the men's institute, and provided with Clare for the order of women, he could fulfill the dream of his first consecration to the Church of Christ by departing to preach the gospel, like the first apostles, to the heathen. So strong was this passion in his entire career that the Church herself in her liturgy has called him the "apostolic man." He thought that an effort should be made to convert the Mohammedans, against whom the Crusaders were striving, by the power of the gospel. After different attempts, it seems certain that this brave follower of the apostles, in the year 1219, actually reached the scene of conflict. No doubt he was saddened by the lack of real Christian virtue among the troops from home. He probably started his work among them. Eventually, however, against all advice, he managed with Brother Illuminato, to pass by his own lines, to cross the open country, and enter the camp of the hostile Saracens. Into the very presence of the Sultan he went, there to plead by interpreter the cause of the Master Whom he so passionately loved. The Sultan listened with respect to him, urged him to pray that

# ST. FRANCIS OF ASSISI

God might show to him what faith was most pleasing to Him, but then sent him back to the camp of the Christians. It seems probable that while in the Holy Land Francis visited the sacred places, perhaps spending Christmas of 1220 in Bethlehem. It appears that the institution of the Christmas crib which came from our Saint is due to this pilgrimage. Francis made other attempts to labor among the heathen, but his real work was at home. This apostolic spirit which burned so strongly within him, was caught by his brethren who manifested their true Catholicism by entering upon the foreign missions. Today that same interest in the pagan portions of the Master's vineyard is alive in his children, some of whom are found in China and Africa.

This noble quality in Francis should bear fruit in every one of us. The Savior died for all. He commanded His apostles to preach to all nations. If we have any of the love that so animated the heart and soul of this Saint, we will bear our share in this glorious work. No real Christian can give a deaf ear to that mandate of the Master, nor to the pleas of millions of souls who are in pagan darkness. By the sweet incense of constant prayer, by the regular contribution of our mite of gold, and in some cases by the heroic sacrifice of self, we shall demonstrate like the Poor Man of Assisi, our apostolic Catholicity, and aid in bearing the light of faith to the heathen.

Called back to guide and govern his brethren, Francis, once again in his native haunts, renewed with his old-time vigor the practice of preaching. While thus engaged he conceived and established what many of his devotees regard the greatest work of his life, the Third Order of Franciscans. To satisfy the thousands of fervent souls who could not give up their station in the world, he instituted this religious order whereby those good Christians, by fulfilling special offices of prayer, works of charity towards the needy, could share in the blessings of the religious life. The Third Order's power and actual accomplishments for the good of the individuals and the rejuvenation of society, cannot be over-estimated. It sanctified the laity in every rank and condition. It was, incidentally, instrumental in abolishing the war-like spirit of the Middle Ages, by its prohibition of engaging in feudal strife. Many of the noblest characters of subsequent generations were proud to be humble members of this religious society, and to be laid out in death in its habit; among them the great and immortal Dante.

The flowering and fruit of that remarkable spirit of brotherly charity that made its appearance in our Saint in even his tender years was evident especially during this period of zeal among the cities and towns of Italy. That extraordinary love of neighbor was, perhaps, the outstanding trait in the make-up of this astounding man of God. It is this quality that is referred to when men today speak of the Franciscan spirit. It was this characteristic which won for him friends when he first took the road to beg his daily bread. It was the same noble virtue of kindliness, of humble devotion to the poor and sick, especially the lepers, which gained for him his first disciples. It was patient acceptance of insults, generosity towards those reviling him, which converted enemies into friends, and resulted in that universal wave of Christian Brotherliness and filial love which was the outstanding effect of the work of Francis in his century and age. No one who reads his life can fail to find therein the most perfect fulfillment of the mandate of the Master to love one another as He has loved us. Because of its acceptance and spread, the world moved in a new way with nobler ideals and happier lives. Francis, in very truth, helped to make the world a better place in which to live. Down through the centuries, this man of God, this great lover of his fellow-man, preaches the same doctrine of charity towards all our brethren in the flesh, and pleads with all who admire his earnestness to forget petty differences

and to have the high-mindedness, the practical
love for every child of God that Christ desired
when He said, "By this shall men know that you
are My disciples: that you have love one for
another."

The sun of Francis' life was now ready to set.
He had been a great and shining light, radiating
the brightness of faith, the splendor of charity,
the excellence of poverty. Like Mary Immaculate,
the Mother of God, to whom he always referred
his undertaking and to whom he directed the
countless hearts to which he preached, Francis
had, in true humility, always sought only the
Word and Will of God. During these late days
internal dissensions broke out, which, in disturbing
his external peace, served also to draw his pure
soul closer, if such were possible, to the passion of
Christ, which had been his refuge and strength
from those early days when he knelt, arms out-
stretched, before the crucifix in his little church at
San Damiano where the Master spoke to the
servant. At that early period, he had formed the
axiom that the essence of true Christianity was the
life of Christ crucified in every one of the faithful.
Now at length, at the sunset of his journey, the
same Loving Savior was to speak to him again,
this time in a manner so vivid and forcible, that
all would admit the sanctity of this extraordinary

soul and the union that existed between the Master and the servant. Francis had gone to a mountain-retreat, Alverno, there to commune with his Divine Friend. With him he had taken a few of the brothers. As Our Lord in the Garden of Gethsemane brought His chosen ones a distance into the garden and then withdrew from even them, so now Francis left these disciples and betook himself to a sequestered hill to spend some time alone with Almighty God. Brother Leo, a comrade from early years, would bring each day a modicum of food and then depart. Thus it was while alone, on the Feast of the Exaltation of the Cross, September 14, 1224, that a strange, a wonderful event occurred. As the angel visited the Master in Gethsemane, so now down from the heights of heaven came an angel to this man of prayer. When the angel had departed the hands and feet and side of Francis, the humble follower of the Crucified, bore visible reproductions of the Five Wounds of Christ. He, who had been so devoted to the Savior received on Mount Alverno divine confirmation of his virtues by this signal visitation and the sacred stigmata. For the rest of his days, he bore upon his flesh this evidence of God's love and this pledge of his union with the Savior of men.

His passing from life to glory was not long

after this miracle at Alverno. For a time, he tried to return to his missionary preaching but the human engine was nigh exhausted. He became blind towards the end of his days and suffered greatly. Everywhere he went, however, he was enthusiastically received, and proclaimed a saint. When it was clear that his end was approaching, he asked to be brought back to Portiuncula, the place of his first love, the Bethlehem of his flourishing order. To be true to the last to his lady poverty, he had himself laid on the bare ground, where amid the singing by his brethren of some of the hymns he had written in praise of the Creator, on October 3, 1226, his soul left its brother-body, and soared to its Heavenly Spouse.

Thus passed one of the greatest as well as the humblest human beings this earth has ever known. "Not since the Savior Himself has there lived a man who has brought to the world so beautiful a message of life, of light, of sweetness and peace as Francis has brought, and the passage of the centuries serves only to emphasize and deepen the effect of his message." Born rich, he became poor for the sake of the Master, Who, though He was God, did not think it robbery to become man. As other youths give their hearts to a maiden, he gave his to the Divine Lover. As a result, the world is richer and nobler. To it he left a heritage

## ST. FRANCIS OF ASSISI

of high ideals and an inviting example. Having grasped the gospel-message in its completeness, he gained life by losing it. His fidelity to the command of the Savior to love one's neighbor as oneself, marks him as one of the truest of Christians. To mankind he has bequeathed a rich legacy of good works, that are even in this distant century bearing fruit. If we, who are subjects of the same Master and Lord, would imitate something of his real charity, if out of love for God, we would make our own lives examples of the love and kindness towards others that Francis of Assisi taught, earth would be brighter and Heaven nearer.

# St. Dominic

IF IT be true as Longfellow says:

"Lives of great men all remind us
We can make our lives sublime,
And departing, leave behind us
Footprints on the sands of time."

then the story of St. Dominic, one of the saints of
the Middle Ages, and the founder of the Dominican Order, should well repay our reading. So
great were his power and influence that the noble
work which he did for the spread of the truth has
increased and magnified itself in the course of the
succeeding centuries. Because of the extraordinary
character of St. Dominic and the popular tendency
of the Middle Ages to deify its heroes, many
legends are intertwined with the truth regarding
the birth of the Saint. He was born about 1170 in
Calaroga in Spain, that country which has given
so many holy men and women to the world. This
town in Calaroga was in the territory so valiantly
sought by the Saracens, and so gallantly saved
finally by the Christians. No doubt the deep love
for the true faith found in Dominic was due in
part to the heavy price that his kinsmen paid to
uphold and retain it. His parents, Felix de Guz-

# ST. DOMINIC

man and Joanna d'Aza, were of noble lineage and
excellent examples of sincere Christian living.
Their home was one of peace and happiness; here
the childhood days of the boy were passed amid
comfort and contentment.

At the age of seven he was sent to his uncle to
commence his education. The latter, arch-priest
at Gumiel d'Izan, could be trusted to guide this
latest vine of the family-tree aright. With other
boys his own age, he would receive from the
Padre a solid training in the rudiments of learning. This period embraced seven years, during
which the boy Dominic, of a serious and studious
disposition, made such progress that at its conclusion he was ready for his higher training. The
interested uncle sent him to the university at
Palencia where he would obtain the course in the
arts and sciences as conducted in the established
institutions of learning throughout all Europe.
The seeds of knowledge scattered here by enthusi-
astic professors found the mind of Dominic rich
soil where they were well nourished and cultivated; thither they would grow to goodly trees
that in due season would bring forth fruit a
hundredfold.

When the young man completed his studies in
the general course, he enrolled for special work in
sacred theology. He was now twenty years of age.

To this chosen field, he devoted himself with all the zest of one destined by God for the priestly rank. Four years were spent in this particular science, and it is said that his books, later sold by him for the relief of the poor, gave ample proof of the attention he focused upon theology. The gentle quiet stream of learning that had its inception at this time in the life of Dominic would develop to a broad deep river that later as a mighty force would purify and irrigate the dry soil of the hearts of men through the entire continent of Europe. It was while thus engaged that his vocation to the priesthood was definitely decided; the product of Sunny Spain where his progenitors had suffered so generously and fought so tirelessly for their religion, had imbibed their Christian spirit and determined to consecrate his talents and ambitions to Almighty God. Just when and how the voice of the Master prevailed upon him is one of the secrets of the King. Perhaps Dominic would say:

"One heard the call and came!
    One heard the whispering of one's name;
One turned away from all the world's fair hopes,
    And pitched one's tent on God's clear mountain slope."

That he was stirred to his very soul by the call, is evident from the life of these student years. While a good friend and companion to all, he was of a

# ST. DOMINIC

serious nature, zealous to prepare himself fittingly
for his work. The moving grace of God was even
now impelling him to charity towards others, especially the poor, to relieve whom he bartered
even his necessary possessions. Realizing also that
the priestly character could only be formed to the
perfect man Christ Jesus by much care and training, he saw to it that these years of study were
also given to prayer and the cultivation of the
virtues so essential for perseverance in the ecclesiastical state.

The exact date of his ordination is not known.
It seems certain that previous to it he held the
position of a canon, *i.e.*, a member of a Cathedral-
choir, whose duty it is to fulfill the office of the
Church at regular hours. While engaged at his
studies, another could be performing this obliga-
tion for him. Probably in 1194 the great day of
his life arrived when he received the power of
God coming upon him, and was enrolled forever
as a priest according to the order of Melchisedech.
That to Dominic this high office was a treasure of
priceless worth, no one can doubt. While it is true,
as Father Russell, S.J. has said so beautifully:

"The world shines bright for inexperienced eyes,
    And death seems distant to the gay and strong.
    And in the youthful heart proud fancies throng,
    And only present good can nature prize,"

our Saint, by the grace of God, cast aside once and forever the call of the world. Once ordained, he gave himself completely to the service of his Master. His fidelity to his duties, his love for the house of God, his zeal for the divine office, his abhorrence of any worldly spirit, his punctuality, his appreciation of the value of time, all these afford meditation for every Christian, particularly for those young men upon whose hands the oil of ordination is still fresh. He could exclaim in all sincerity, "I have loved, O Lord, the beauty of Thy house and the place where Thy glory dwelleth!" To the prior of the Cathedral-Chapter at Osma, whither Dominic went to take up his obligations, these qualities gave great satisfaction. To that holy man, desirous of conforming the standards of the canons to the ideals expressed by the various popes and the present bishop, the conduct of this young levite was especially consoling and gratifying. It was only natural, therefore, that when the bishop died and the prior was chosen for his see, the latter appointed Dominic to fill the post of prior of the Chapter of the Cathedral. Some have fancied pleasing stories of these nine years of his service as prior; the truth, however, seems to be that they were uneventful, devoted perseveringly to his Cathedral duties, in which he offered unostentatious example of fidelity to those about him.

In the year 1203 by God's providence, our Saint was unknowingly directed to his particular labor in the vineyard of the Lord. Little did he realize when asked by the bishop to accompany him on an embassy for the king that God was manifesting the work laid out for him for all eternity. So it is with every one of us. One fails to appreciate that God acts through natural channels. One seldom perceives what mighty destinies are in the balance, what accomplishments for God's glory and our fellow-man's salvation, depend on the response to some trivial invitation. The task of the bishop was to seek the hand of a noble lady for the King's son. Where the lady lived is unimportant; what is of consequence is that Bishop Didacus and Dominic passed through the country of Toulouse in France, and observed there the miserable state of Christianity because of the evils inflicted by the insidious and devastating Albigensian heresy.

This heresy, also called the Waldensian or the Catharist, was essentially a social one. "It denied the doctrines, hierarchy and worship of the Catholic Church, as well as the essential rights of the State." "Not only were the Cathari hostile to the church and her divine worship, but they were also

in open revolt against the State and its rights."
"Some of them not only disputed the lawfulness
of taxation, but went so far as to condone stealing
provided the thief did no injury to the believers.
War, according to them, could never be lawful.
'In no instance,' they said, 'has one the right to
kill another; neither the internal welfare of a
country nor its external interests can justify mur-
der.' The soldier defending his country is as much
a murderer as the most common criminal."*

The sincere, zealous Dominic, face to face with
the wretched situation, saw that here was real
work for the Kingdom of God. Obedient to the
voice of the Savior, he thought no more of return-
ing to his native Spain. The bishop and he decided
to give themselves whole-heartedly to this field
which was to prove the proper vocation of the latter, and in the plan of God, the stepping-stone to
greater work for his Master. It is here one sees
the real Dominic, truly apostolic, an example and
inspiration to every Christian. With Bishop
Didacus he went to Citeaux to place himself under
the Cistercians who were conducting a preaching
crusade against the deluded heretics. The two new
recruits would be found later greater than their
teachers. The good bishop would bear the burdens
for two years like the simplest priest. Dominic,

*Quotations from Vacandard, *The Inquisition.*

# ST. DOMINIC

young and vigorous, would stay in this mission for
ten years.

The latter saw, at the outset, the need of apostolic poverty if any impression was to be made.
These heretics were insisting on unworldliness.
For them it was the touchstone of orthodoxy. The
misguided Cistercians, with their splendid equip-
age to carry them through the heretical country,
were merely affording targets for the criticism of
the Catharist leaders. Dominic traveled on foot
and met the populace, engaging in conversation
with the peasants. His food was the same or even
poorer and far scantier than theirs, his bed generally the roadside. In many respects he was another St. Paul. His whole attitude said, "I seek
not yours but you." This humble appearance won
for him attention. His powerful preaching gained
for him adherents. Man of God that he was, he
brought the misled people, in many cases, to their
senses. While he was not always victorious, the
success that often accompanied his discourses was
discouraging to the preachers of infidelity. His
conduct could not be impugned; his logic and elo-
quence were inimitable. If, when he engaged his
opponents in public debate, he did not convert the
hearers, he left them usually convinced of the
emptiness of the heretical doctrines. This was al-

35

ways true: wherever this new preacher went, conversions from all classes resulted.

The difficulties that Dominic encountered cannot be passed over. The wrath of the false teachers who now had a worthy, unimpeachable antagonist, could not be bridled. When honest souls turned from heresy to the truth, plots were laid to get our Saint out of the way. It was only when the opposition became convinced of his disdain of all suffering that they decided it would be the summit of folly to satisfy one who longed for martyrdom so sincerely and ardently. Dominic could truly have said:

> "Better a day of strife
> Than a century of sleep;
> Give me instead of a long stream of life
> The tempest and tears of the deep."

Once some of these malicious conspirators asked him, "Dost thou not fear death? What wouldst thou do were we to lay hands on thee?" The crushing reply was: "I would entreat you not to put me to death at once, but to tear me from limb to limb so as to prolong my martyrdom. I would fain remain a dismembered trunk, have my eyes torn out, be covered with blood, in order at last to wear a fair martyr's crown." What sturdy faith of our Saint! What genuine contempt of this life! What real yearning "To be dissolved and to be with Christ." At least, our faith should make us hate what offends God and be anxious to convert others even at much sacrifice. He reminds one of that spiritual giant, Ignatius Martyr, whose words perhaps had provided him in the past with meditations: "Leave me to become the food of beasts that I may become worthy of God. I am the wheat of God and by the teeth of wild beasts I shall be ground that I may be found the pure bread of God." "Fire and the cross and the beasts are prepared, cutting off the limbs, and the scattering of the bones and crushing of the whole body; harsh torments of the devil, let these come upon me, but only let me be accounted worthy of Jesus Christ." Would that the same desire to be true to God were in every Christian soul! How the Church would shine in splendor as the immaculate bride of Christ. One can understand the success that attended St. Dominic's efforts.

While traveling through the different provinces, our Missionary came in contact with the various organizations for the suppression of heresy and also with the militant crusaders bent on checking these foes of the civil power as well as of religion. Simon de Montfort, the illustrious leader of the armed forces, whose name is found again and again in the accounts of the struggles in Southern France, very early conceived a liking for

Dominic. Many times they had occasion to meet; always the friendship increased. Because of this intimacy with one so actively identified with the aggressive, militant pursuit of the Albigenses, some have asserted that our Saint was a partner in the bloody work of Simon. The subject, including the Inquisition, is too extensive to be brought in here. The words of such a critical and fair-minded historian as Jean Guiraud should give sufficient light on this vexing question. "Placing the saint in his own age and environment, and taking above all the character of his opponents into consideration, he appears to have been a defender, wise and temperate, not only of faith and morals, but also of civilization threatened as it was by the subversive doctrines of the Albigenses."

Over and above the force of the preaching of St. Dominic was the power of his example. This was a weapon, the influence of which cannot be over-estimated. It was what was lacking in the missionaries who had conducted the spiritual campaign previous to our Saint. Plutarch has said, "Moral good is a practical stimulus; it is no sooner seen than it inspires an impulse to practice." Everywhere Dominic's sincerity, his whole-hearted interest in the things of God, moved the well-intentioned people. His deportment was an argument that the heretical leaders could not

answer. To see this Priest surrendering all the
comforts and conveniences of the world, living as
the humblest peasant, was a sermon, the effect of
which was incomparable. His imitation of apostolic poverty: sleeping in the open air at night and
journeying barefoot from town to town, forced
the skeptical populace to acknowledge that here
was a man of God. This good example was far-
reaching in its effects. It gained an audience and
favor where the Cistercians had been insulted and
repulsed. This silent influence found its way so
deeply into the hearts of the rank and file that the
number cannot be computed who accepted the
doctrine of this zealous preacher and returned
to the Church that sponsored and nourished such
a learnèd and holy man.

That the blessing of God in the form of miracles accompanied the labors of this great character, cannot be doubted. In the lives of the saints
of the Middle Ages one has to be prudent in
accepting accounts of prodigies because of the
tendency on the part of contemporaries and
immediate followers to add lustre to those admired. There are certain miracles of Dominic,
however, so well-authenticated that it would be
unreasonable to disregard them. One such is
narrated by his first biographer, Jordan of
Saxony, his successor as Master General of the

# HERALDS OF THE KING

Order of Preachers. "It chanced that a conference was held at Fanjeaux, in the presence of a multitude of the faithful and unfaithful who had been summoned thither. The Catholics had prepared several memoranda containing reasons and authorities in support of their faith. But, after a comparison of them, they gave the preference to the one written by the blessèd servant of God, Dominic, and determined to oppose it to that of the heretics. Three arbitrators were chosen by common consent to judge to which party belonged the best arguments and the most solid faith. Now when after much talk these arbitrators could not agree together, the idea occurred to them to cast the two memoranda into the fire, so that, should one of them be spared by the flames, it might be certain that it contained the true doctrine of faith. A great fire is, therefore, lighted and the two volumes are cast into it; that of the heretics is consumed; the other, written by the blessèd servant of God, Dominic, not only remains intact, but is thrown forth by the flames in the presence of the noble assembly. A second and third time it is cast into the fire; a second and third time the result is the same, manifesting clearly on which side lies the truth and testifying to the holiness of him by whom the book was written."

Dominic had not been a long time laboring

among these people when he realized the necessity of enrolling women in his cause in an organized way if his efforts were to have lasting results. As in our own age the power and influence of the gentler sex is being constantly employed in all kinds of propaganda, so at this time throughout Languedoc the women were efficient auxiliaries of the men, even in certain localities the very backbone of the heresy. Our Saint concluded that he must adopt the successful means of the enemy, establish some institution of women to possess their co-operation and to provide an outlet for their interest and zeal. Moreover, if some of the women won from the Albigenses were to persevere, there must be an institution where they would be protected, and could likewise contribute to the conversion of others. The paramount question was material, a convent where such as desired could live a common life dedicated completely to the service of God. Tradition manifests that this was answered by a miracle. While Dominic was praying for guidance to the Mother of God, to whom he always had a strong devotion, a globe of light appeared over the abandoned church of Prouille. Three times this phenomenon occurred so that he saw in it a sign from heaven. There he would establish the convent for these converted, zealous women. Having obtained title from Foulques, the bishop, he placed the building in order, gave it the title, "Our Lady of Prouille" and brought thither nine women desirous of consecrating themselves to God. This all took place in 1206. It marked the commencement of the Cloistered Nuns of the Dominican Order who have since been so precious in the sight of God.

Dominic naturally was their director. The nuns spent their time in spiritual exercises and manual labor in the monastery since they were cloistered. Other women now joined the happy community, which observed at the suggestion of Dominic, the rule of St. Augustine. Benefactors came forward to show their interest and appreciation. Many temporal princes were lavish with their donations, particularly Simon de Montfort. To ensure the full possession of their rights and property, Dominic in 1215 obtained from Pope Innocent III canonical approval and protection for the new order. Succeeding popes added to the privileges thus granted.

With the order of women an accomplished fact, the practical mind of our Saint gave attention to the evident need of a preaching order of priests to cope more systematically and extensively with the immediate conditions in France and to aid the Church in other fields. As Father Hecker, the Paulist, aptly said, "The lone fisherman may

# ST. DOMINIC

catch a few fish for amusement with a rod, but the fisherman who makes a living at the business uses a net." Attracted by his whole-hearted abandonment of self, his ardent zeal for the cause of Christ, and his particular genius for directing others, the little band of preachers who had followed Bishop Didacus had already placed themselves under Dominic. The Bishop of Toulouse, Foulques, an exemplary prelate, had gladly accepted this group as a religious order in his diocese. To gain for it the approval of the Head of the Church was a more difficult task. The mind of Rome was, in fact, set against new orders. Hence, although our Saint went to the Lateran Council in 1215 to obtain official recognition and sanction, he was unsuccessful. Genuinely convinced, however, that there was need of such an order not only as an aid to the extirpation of heresy, but also to teach the truths revealed by Christ throughout the length and breadth of Europe, Saint Dominic with that sublime faith in Almighty God which should be an inspiration to all not to admit defeat, decided that the order should accept the long-approved rule of St. Augustine. When his confreres agreed to this he returned to Rome to renew his plea. His perfect faith was rewarded. Pope Honorius III, in the year 1216, canonically recognized and took under his special patronage this new institute, referring to its members as "champions of the faith and true lights of the church." Dominic's dream of eleven years was now a reality; the Order of Preaching Friars would sow the seeds of Christian knowledge and virtue, would enkindle the flickering flames of revealed religion, would hold aloft and cause to burn more brightly the torch of learning; here was an order from which would spring ardent apostles to be witnesses unto Christ, dispensers of the mysteries of God, not only in Southern France but all over the world.

There are some legends regarding the establishment of the order, which if not true, certainly are fanciful. According to one, Innocent III, Pope at the time of the Lateran Council, saw in his sleep the great Lateran Church, the mother of all churches, rent and crumbling. He then saw Dominic come, place himself against the church, thus supporting and strengthening it. At first fright-ened, Innocent afterward perceived the meaning of the vision. He sent for the Saint, told him to accept the rule of St. Augustine and that he would receive approval.

Another story is that while Dominic was praying in the Bascilica of St. Peter, he had a vision; "he seemed to perceive the Lord Jesus in the air brandishing three lances against the world. Immediately the Virgin Mary throws herself at His feet, conjuring Him to show mercy to those whom He has purchased, and thus to temper justice with pity. Her Son replies, 'Seest thou not the outrages they lavish upon Me? My justice cannot leave unpunished such great evils.' And His Mother answers, 'Thou art not ignorant, My Son,—Thou to Whom all is known,—that there is a means of recalling them to Thyself. I have a faithful servant; send him to proclaim Thy word to them, and they will be converted and will seek after Thee, the Savior of all. For his assistance I will give him another of my servants who will work in a like way.' The Son says to His Mother: 'I have heard Thy prayer. Show Me whom Thou has destined to such an office.' And she straightway presents to Him the Blessèd Dominic. 'He will perform well,' says the Savior, 'and zealously that which Thou hast said.' Mary then offers to Him the blessèd Francis, and the Savior commends him after the same manner. At this moment Dominic looks with attention at his companion, with whom hitherto he was not acquainted; and on the morrow finding in a church him whom he had seen in the night, he hastens towards him and pressing him in his arms, says: 'Thou shalt be my comrade; thou shalt be with me. Let us remain together and no enemy shall prevail over us.' Then he confides to him the vision that he has had, and thenceforth they were but one heart and one soul in Christ, directing their children to observe the same forever."

It is important to see the lines on which our Saint laid this order destined to accomplish much good. The outstanding mark was poverty. The object was to avoid completely the luxurious spirit of the age which was responsible for many of its sins. Dominic wanted missionaries who had renounced everything the world offers. No property could be possessed. The friars would live as the poorest peasants. Their dress would be common, their food coarse, their journeys on foot. Herein is a needed suggestion in this present age of luxury. As the Son of God rejected the goods of this world when tempted by Satan, as He embraced and pursued a life of simplicity, Christians, His children and followers, should never allow the good things of the world to draw them away from Almighty God. Very seldom do riches and luxury bring one nearer to heaven; too often they are a stumbling-block. Dominic's example should prompt all to imitate him at least to the extent of avoiding any excess that would compromise them in their love and zeal for the Master.

The great, all-important duty of the Dominicans was preaching. If religion was suffering, it

was because the people had not received the bread
of life, the word of God. As the snow melts under
the gentle influence of the warm sun, so would the
crust of infidelity disappear under the persuasive
power of the teachings of the Savior. Christ has
said, "Preach the gospel." Our Saint, early in his
ministry, perceived that the neglect of this was
responsible for much of the leakage from the
Church. He also saw that a superficial knowledge
of religion would not suffice. Men had to be told
the reason of the faith, the necessity of fidelity to
the organization Christ had founded and the
power it possessed for the soul's sanctification.
The pure gold of Christian doctrine would enrich
the beggared lives of men. This sacred love for
the truths of God and this filial fidelity to the
Church established by the Divine Savior should be
awakened and encouraged likewise in the world
today. Dominic clearly saw that the Catholic
Church was the only institution that had a vital,
satisfying message for the starving minds of men.
She alone has real truth to impart. His experience
convinced him that Christians lacked a sound
knowledge of her teachings, and as a consequence,
were in many places too indifferent in their attach-
ment to her. The keen intelligence of our Apostle
grasped the need of the times: preachers who
would set forth in its completeness and beauty and

power the philosophy of life expounded by the
Son of God. The seeds of Christian doctrine sown
in his monasteries would there be nourished and
developed, and when strong and healthy, transplanted into the soil of all Europe. The wisdom of
the man was proved by the response to the work
of his friars. If the same church is to be a source
of power in this age, the same means must be employed. A comprehensive knowledge of their religion must be implanted and developed in the
minds of Christians. The laity must be drawn into
a closer bond with the Church in order that they
may be prepared to carry into the world fearlessly
and valiantly the principles that alone can insure
its salvation.

To see the fullness of this spiritual and social
development according to the idea of Dominic,
one must know something of the Dominican Third
Order. Its object was to satisfy the longing of
those living in the world for a more intimate union
with the Divine Lover, to afford them a more
active participation in the blessings and consola-
tions that religion offers, and to allow them to
assume a larger share in the Church's mission of
increasing and enriching the kingdom of God on
earth. Men and women from all spheres of society
flocked to this organization. As some peaceful
rivulet starting calmly in the mountain-recesses

gains in width and proportion gradually as it descends until it is a mighty stream carrying in its current giant logs and massive boulders, so this soul-comforting movement began imperceptibly, growing gradually until it attracted attention as a powerful force carrying kings and queens, artisans and scholars in its embrace. Back of it was the same idea that Pius XI is inculcating when he speaks of Catholic Action, *viz.* a fuller development of the Christian life. The tertiary had his badge as the preacher and nun had their respective habits; indeed, the tertiary wore the scapular as the essence of the religious habit. He had his particular religious practices that tended to the cultivation of the mystical spirit; he followed certain exercises of mortification and penance as atonements for the evils of men and also to check any inclination to imitate pagan principles. This Third Order was in very truth like a golden chain uniting in one bond countless souls in the world and binding them in loving servitude to the feet of God. To quote Lacordaire, "The history of this institution is as beautiful as anything ever written. It produced saints in every walk of life from the throne to the footstool in such abundance that the cloister and the wilderness might well be jealous." It should be the ambition and aim of every member of the Church to have the same love for

49

Christ and religion, the same spirit of prayer, and the same interest in the conversion of others.

Dominic could now feel that he had set in motion a plan which in his early years he had formed for the salvation of the Church. He had seen while in Languedoc a vision of a new, invigorated Europe, and that vision was now a reality. His preachers, well trained in theology, had been directed, after the recognition of the order by Rome, to all parts of Europe. Provinces had been established in Rome, Lombardy, Spain, Provence, France, Germany, Hungary and England. The friars, because so efficiently taught in their monasteries, where deep study was individually cultivated under their brethren who were formerly professors in the most renowned universities, would bear the good tidings to the children of men. The Sisters, first established at Prouille in France, were now joined with others in Rome and other parts of Italy, due to the appreciation of the popes of this necessary work, and the zeal of Dominic for the nuns who required a rule with loftier ideals to guide their aspirations. The Third Order, continually growing in numbers and fervor, was proving the leaven to raise society to the stature intended by the God-Man.

All three organizations fostered in a gratifying way that tender and deep reverence and love for

the Mother of God that was so evident in the life
of their founder. Nothing gives a better idea of
his Catholic spirit than this filial confidence and
devotion. As the North Star, never setting, ever
directs and reassures the mariner observing it, so
Mary, never failing, ever guided and strengthened Dominic, always loyal to this Bright Star of
Heaven. It protected his younger years against
the temptations of student life and drew him
closer to the Divine Son while a canon at Osma.
Amid the discouragements and dangers in Languedoc, this union with God's Mother nourished
and strengthened his faith and ardor. When the
delicate and weighty question of an institute for
the women converted was perplexing his mind, it
was to Our Lady he went, and it was she who,
according to a well-founded tradition, pointed out
to him on three successive days the place for a
convent. Thus it was that his first convent was
dedicated to Our Lady of Prouille. When similar
problems arose regarding the Order of Preachers,
it was the Mother of God who directed the plans
to a satisfactory conclusion. That same love and
interest in all that concerns Mary has manifested
itself wherever the sons and daughters of Dominic have set foot and the Queen of Heaven has
been the spiritual sword warding off from them
all dangers.

# HERALDS OF THE KING

Another saint whose love was cherished by Dominic, one who also was devoted to Mary, was Francis of Assisi. The friendship between these two great men of God is one of the most interesting incidents in the story of the Church. Both were extraordinary, both were little in their own eyes and great before God and men. Where the acquaintance first began cannot be traced. It is certain, however, that the friendship became strong and lasting, that it redounded to the benefit not only of themselves, but also to their spiritual sons and daughters, and what is more, to the glory of the universal Church.

Zealous Apostle that he was, Dominic, now that his religious institutes were functioning, determined that the time was ripe for him to fulfill the desire of his heart, that was to devote his energies to the conversion of the barbarous Tartars. This marvelous man, intimate friend and adviser of popes and temporal lords, desired now only to lose his personality in the arduous labor of evangelizing the heathen. The humility of the man exceeded even his natural talents. This task and mission, in the plan of Almighty God, would, however, be left to his children in religion. They would fulfill this yearning of his apostolic soul which he would not carry out while on earth. The latest flowering and fruit of that seed imbedded

ST. DOMINIC

in the heart of this champion of Christ is the Foreign Mission Sisters of St. Dominic at Maryknoll,
New York.

Dominic, though young as men's lives go, had
accomplished much in a short time and Heaven
was already summoning him to bestow a crown of
imperishable glory. In accordance with an agree-
ment at the Chapter of Bologna, in 1220, he
returned the following year for the Second General Chapter of Friars Preachers. When he arrived it was clear that his work in this world was
almost completed. Sickness had wasted his
strength, fever had sapped his strong constitution.
Human aid was powerless to hold on earth him
who had such a right to heaven. He realized even
better than the brethren his condition and did not
demur. From the moment when he first put his
hand to the plow he had spent himself unselfishly
for God. Over and over again as he journeyed
first through Languedoc, later through all Europe, his noble spirit must have cried out:

> "Oh give my youth, my faith, my sword,
>   Choice of the heart's desire.
> A short life in the saddle, Lord!
>   Not long life by the fire."

The time left was divided between prayer and
instructions to the brethren to be faithful to the
ideals and rules of the Order. Poverty was espe-

cially enjoined upon them since it had been instrumental in winning the respect of the people, and drawing them from the world to God. On the Feast of the Transfiguration, amid the tears and prayers of the assembled religious, the soul of this noble champion of Christ's cause, this valiant servant of God, was released from its prison to enjoy forever the vision that the favored apostles saw only for an instant on Mount Tabor. Only thirteen years later, because of the well-attested holiness of his life and the numerous authenticated miracles worked through intercession to him, Pope Gregory IX, Dominic's personal friend, formerly Cardinal Ugolino, declared him a saint of the Church he had served so conscientiously.

Such was a fitting close to the earthly career of this extraordinary man whose span had reached only fifty years. In all humility he could have said, "For this was I born, and for this came I into the world: that I might give testimony to the truth." "I have glorified Thee, Father, on earth: I have finished the work Thou gavest me to do." In the same number of years others had laid only the foundation of their work; Dominic, in all confidence, could sing his "Nunc Dimittis,"—"Now dost Thou dismiss Thy servant, O Lord, in peace." Some pioneers, like Moses, are not allowed to see the promised land whither their

# ST. DOMINIC

steps have tended. Dominic, dying at fifty years, not only had sown the seed, but like Patrick in Ireland, lived to see the fruit and the gathering of the harvest. He departed from this earth serene and content, leaving behind him an army of children to perpetuate his name, to carry on his work,—religious men and women,—as well as a fervent lay-order that would live for God while toiling in the world. These three trees which he planted, tended and nourished, would, though he was gone, continue to spread their branches, blossom with new foliage, and would provide shade, shelter and refreshment to the sons of men.

The spirit that animated St. Dominic should prevail today, not only among his own spiritual descendants who are worthily holding aloft the torch of learning and zealously propagating the truth by preaching and prayer, but among all members of the Church which he loved so earnestly, and which gave official approval to his accomplishments. That ardent adherence to every dogma of Christ which made him ready to die at the hands of the heretics is necessary in this age when false and shallow philosophy is striking at the core of civilization. The intelligent desire to know more thoroughly our religion will stimulate us to be valiant champions of truth and light against error and darkness. His appreciation of

# HERALDS OF THE KING

the power of good example and sound Christian life will in this epoch bring about many conversions to Catholicism. Under the ægis of the glorious St. Dominic, those who are still in the darkness and shadow of death will enter the portals of that Church where dwells Jesus Christ, and Mary, His Mother.

# St. Ignatius Loyola

THESE SUBLIME and impressive lines of Alfred Lord Tennyson:

"I held it truth, with him who sings
To one clear harp in divers tones,
That men may rise on stepping-stones
Of their dead selves to higher things,"

find justification in the story of one of the strongest characters in world history, and one of the noblest saints of the Catholic Church, Ignatius Loyola. Merely to glance at his life, brings home the truth of the poet's words. The career of this man, which developed so gloriously for himself and the world, is an example of the power that even one good and zealous person can exercise in a corrupt age. The way that he changed his allegiance from earthly ends to heavenly ones, bringing into play the very talents that were intended to serve to advance him in the court and the army, is a sermon to all willing to read it. His biography should be interesting to men today because he had and employed those very qualities that are successful in big business. These characteristics he made use of to win his associates to his principles in order to further the glory of God and the welfare of society and civilization. If he were being appraised in this era of collective enterprise, he would be acclaimed a great executive, a captain of men, a directive genius.

Coming into an atmosphere that was charged with rebellion, and infiltrated with license and luxury, partaking in his early years of its spirit, Ignatius, the one-time cavalier, by complete self-immolation, effected first in himself, then in society at large, a moral transformation that can be regarded as nothing less than a miracle. No one who pretends to education can afford to be ignorant of his life-story, or the influence that he exerted upon the unique century of the Protestant Revolution. In an age, moreover, when efficiency is deified, when organization is the talisman and hall-mark of success, the work of Ignatius Loyola, who through these means achieved astounding, incredible results, must be studied by those who hope to sway the minds of others. What is more, if honorable and intelligent souls are sincerely concerned about the civilization of the present, aware of the social evils that threaten, and searching for a sensible method to attack them, they should pay court to this extraordinary character who acted such a prominent part in the drama of the sixteenth century.

It is worth remembering that the child who

# ST. IGNATIUS LOYOLA

was to have such an influence in defending the
Catholic religion was born in the same year, 1491,
as the future Henry VIII, of England, who was
to cause it such keen sorrow. Ignatius was, therefore, only a year old when Columbus opened the
way to a new continent. His ancestral home was in
the little town of Loyola, in the Basque country
of Spain, not far from the Pyrenees. His parents,
Don Beltrán Yáñez de Oñez e Loyola and Doña
Maria Saenz de Licona y Balda, were of noble
blood, and true to its finest traditions. They were
blessed with thirteen children, the youngest of
eight boys, be it remarked, being the one who
brought glory and immortality to the family name.
He was baptized Inigo; later he took the name
Ignatius, probably through devotion to Ignatius
Martyr. When the boy was very young the father
entrusted him to a kinsman who lived at court
who promised to provide a career for this relative. With this man, therefore, our Saint stayed
until he was twenty-six years old, at which time
unfortunately, as it then seemed, the benefactor
died.

Undeterred by such adversity, the scion of
Loyola, spurred on by the thought of the noble
blood that he inherited, sought a place at court
that he might fulfill his pressing ambition to be a
knight of great Spain and win glory for himself.
Through the impression he had already created,

59

he obtained a post in the retinue of the Duke of Navarre, one of the powerful lords of the time. It was in the latter's forced absence that opportunity came to the energetic Ignatius. Francis I of France was moving against the territory of Navarre. While the duke was seeking aid the citadel at Pamplona was besieged. The commandant, because of his small force, was for surrender, but the valiant noble Loyola demurred and prevailed. During the artillery engagement that followed a cannon ball bruised one leg of Ignatius and shattered the other. With him *hors de combat* the garrison immediately sought terms. In admiration of his courage the enemy carried him to Pamplona for treatment and then permitted him to be sent to the castle at Loyola.

The ardent and ambitious cavalier was now to experience a series of setbacks and incidentally find his destiny. If he could have seen the future he might have exclaimed with Francis Thompson:

> "Ah, must—
> Designer Infinite!—
> Ah, must Thou char the wood ere Thou canst
> limn with it?"

The seriousness of the injury, which had been badly set at Pamplona, caused much suffering. So alarming did his condition seem that the doctors gave up hope and the priest anointed the dying soldier. Tradition narrates that at this turn the young knight appealed to St. Peter whose feast was on the morrow. At any rate, he had a change for the better. When his condition looked favorable, the surgeon announced that another cutting would be necessary if the patient wished to avoid a very noticeable deformity. Afire with ideas of a glorious career in society and the world, the iron will of Ignatius commanded resignation to the agonizing operation. While convalescing, he asked for a good novel. The nearest answer that the stern Spanish household was able to offer was a life of Christ, and a volume on the saints. Unaware of any danger to his plans, he perused what was offered. If he only knew that someone said, "Let me control a people's literature and I will govern their souls." The reading of the life of the "King of Kings" made an unexpected impression on this soldier. Likewise the devotion of the followers of the King, and their heroic achievements. Ignatius reflected how he had always dreamed of being loyal to a leader, of fighting for the honor of his king, of advancing his interests. Here was the Supreme General of all history with some of His captains. Could he serve a nobler master than Christ? Would he be more courageous than these saints? Like Columbus, Loyola had stumbled upon a new world without realizing it. His earthly mind then recalled the sweet pleasures of court, the company of handsome women, the fair one whom he liked to call his own. Perhaps he then happened upon those stirring words of St. Augustine:

> "O Beauty ever ancient, ever new,
> Too late have I known Thee, too late have
> I loved Thee."

Through some such way the grace of God prevailed: adversity had won another yeoman for Jesus Christ.

This determined man entered upon his new project as soon as possible. He believed that life consisted in motion. Surely the inner soul was murmuring, "I have rejoiced in the things which have been said to me; I will go into the house of the Lord." Against the wishes of his eldest brother, who observed with displeasure the conversion, Ignatius left the castle and directed his footsteps towards Montserrat to a famous shrine of the Mother of God.—Act of solid wisdom for a neophyte. St. Matthew narrates of the wise men, "They found the Child with Mary, His Mother." (2:11).

This conversion of Ignatius, a result of mature deliberation, provides material for reflection. From a dandy in the world, he turned to become

ST. IGNATIUS LOYOLA

a follower of Christ. With all the influence that
his previous environment had upon him, although
his health was approaching normal, he forsook
his worldly ambitions to be in the ranks of the
Eternal Commander. Study convinced this man of
passion, of human love, thirsting for companion-
ship and glory, of the nobility of surrendering all
for the humble self-crucifying service of Christ.
This turnabout should at least touch the surface
of the souls of others. Many are not loyal to
themselves or their Maker. Few are giving to God
what is His bounden share. Meanwhile the world
is suffering for the want of characters formed and
governed by the sound principles of the gospel.
Civilization is perishing because the leaven of
Christian truth does not permeate it. Today when
irreverence and materialism are like corrosives
eating out the very foundations of society, there
is a demand for men and women who will see the
wisdom of working hand in hand with the world's
Savior. This generous step by Loyola should
prompt many to take a more active interest in the
organizations sponsored by religion for man's
welfare. It may be the means to awaken a new
enthusiasm in some for the spread of Christian
doctrine and the advancement of true morality.
What a blessing if through the intercession of St.

# HERALDS OF THE KING

Ignatius some souls would today offer their ambitions for the honor of Christ, the King.

The popular Shrine of the Virgin at Montserrat was to serve as the trysting place of our
cavalier and his new Ideal. He was laying his
foundation well; the Mother was to be his pat-
roness before her Divine Son. This was March,
1522. The spirit of the world's chivalry still
directed him. He often had read of the young
knights spending the entire night in vigil with
their arms before entering upon their exploits.
Therefore placing his weapons before Mary's
altar, he passed the vigil of the beautiful feast of
the Annunciation in prayer and meditation.
Thoughts such as these must have burned within
that noble soul:

> "Lady, I would be thy knight,
>     Courting pains and death;
> Blazoning thy honor bright
>     Till my latest breath.
> Ah, sweet Layde, though they leave me
>     Dead upon the field,
> Happy knight, if thou receive me
>     Home, upon my shield."
>                     *(Father Blunt)*

While at this holy place, he stripped his soul of
its worldly vestures by a general confession, and
his body of its proud trappings by an interchange
with a beggar.

64

## ST. IGNATIUS LOYOLA

Thus prepared, he left for the neighboring town of Manresa which was to be his desert of Judea. He had determined to spend a year here in prayer and penance. Concealing his identity, he sought for shelter in the hospital of St. Lucy. Here he soon found employment in visiting the patients. The way he tended the most unfortunate, bathing their wounds, comforting their souls, was a sermon to all. This work, however, occupied only a portion of his time. Outside the city he found an abandoned cave which he adopted for his hermitage. He made it an absolute rule to spend here at least seven hours each day in meditation. Whatever other time he could spare, he gave to begging in the streets for the poor. This might seem a strenuous program but Ignatius had enlisted in the army of Christ. The saints of whom he had read were his exemplars. He would rival not one but all in devotion to the Supreme General. No soldier would be so attached to the flag of his country as Ignatius to the cross of his Savior. Suffering was part of the contract; he was ready for it. In his untaught way he understood that—

> "Who'd tread the god-won heights must fare
>   In the piteous steps of the Crucified;
> The Cross is his to lift and bear;
>   The naked shame, the spear-torn side."

His quiet, unobtrusive charity was an inspiration to others. These Spanish citizens were reminded of the forgotten words of the gospel: "By this shall all men know that you are my disciples, if you have love one for another."

A severe trial came to disrupt the soul of Ignatius in the midst of his devoted days of prayer, penance, and fraternal charity. To dispel his inward peace, to scatter the gathered jewels of contemplation, there descends upon his soul like a plague of locusts, the dread, devastating disease of scrupulosity. As is always the case, the cause could not be established. Perhaps it was his introspection, his too severe fasting, or even his too ambitious program while still a novice in the spiritual life. The effect, in any case, was the banishment of all mental balance. The more he endeavored to probe for the evil, the worse became his disorder. His salvation seemed futile, and prayer useless. So distraught was he when he obtained no certainty or peace that he felt in his inmost being:

"The wine of life is spilled upon the sand.
My heart is as some famine-murdered land
   Whence all good things have perished utterly,
   And well I know my soul in Hell must lie
If I this night before God's throne should stand."

He would have died of starvation in his effort to

drive out the demon if some good people had not
located him in the cave and arranged for his trans-
fer to the Dominican monastery. However, "the
night is long that never finds a day." Finally the
storm scattered itself, the bright sunshine once
more flooded his soul, and he was able to renew
his former devotion. This sourging ordeal was of
great assistance in his later life. He knew the
plight of souls similarly tried, how to sympathize
with them, and the need of divine patience in
confessors.

The marvelous progress that he now made in
the truths of God is an indication of the favors
that he received from heaven. He was giving himself in an extraordinary degree to the Master; in
return he was visited with a special enlightenment
from above. The famous revelation at the bank of
the river Cardoner occurred at this time. Ignatius
later claimed that in this and other visions truths
hidden from the world were revealed to his soul.
What seems to be certain is that during this period
the basic meditations of the famous spiritual exercises were composed. This set of meditations,
which drew his own soul into intimate union with
the Creator, and which was of such advantage for
his religious order, was the fruit of Manresa.

The entire world owes a debt to this Spanish
soldier and mystic for the Spiritual Exercises.

Briefly they are a series of reflections and conferences upon the relation of the individual to his God. They really embody a philosophy of life. It was clear to this former habitat of the royal court that "With desolation is the whole land made desolate because no one thinketh in his heart." He evolved this course of soul-education. The candidate in silence and solitude, went through these exercises under the guidance of a director and considered the logical conclusions deduced therefrom. This devotion was the bait that Ignatius employed to win men from worldly pursuits to the kingdom of God. By the use of them he obtained his first and most devoted followers. He ordained that in his institute all candidates must pass through this test. His sons kept to his legislation with the result that they have been men of keen intellect, iron will, and generous soul.

To Ignatius belongs the credit for the wonderful effects in the universal church through the employment of these exercises under the popular name of missions or retreats. The Jesuits were the originators of these stirring devotions. To their founder must be attributed the benefits brought to the individuals and the communities. In modern times they are being conducted systematically in houses of religion for the laity. These are as it were reservoirs of religion where men, exhausted by contact with the sordid ideals of corrupt society, can find peace of heart, and rejuvenation of spirit. Many a successful business man has breathed a prayer of gratitude to Ignatius Loyola for the institution of these saving exercises. It is greatly desired that many more avail themselves of this means of relaxation and spiritual rebirth. Assuredly particular blessings descend from heaven upon all religious who institute and foster this work so successfully undertaken by Ignatius.

By February, 1523, Ignatius was ready to leave Manresa to take the second step he had planned while sick at his brother's castle. It was his earnest desire to make a pilgrimage to the Holy Land. Deep, fervent love prompted him to wash away the stains of his transgressions in the land where his Liege-Lord had shed His Sacred Blood. He journeyed, therefore, to Barcelona, and sailed from there to Rome where he was obliged to obtain from the Pope a pilgrim's license. After many crosses and sufferings, cheerfully received and borne, he reached Venice, the sailing port for Palestine. Through the Christian charity of some of his fellow-countrymen, who found him getting what sleep he could in the open in the plaza of St. Mark, he obtained passage for Cyprus. It was while at Venice that he said to a well-meaning

Spaniard, who warned him of the dangers of the
voyage because of the hostile Turks, "I have such
confidence in God, our Savior, that, if this year
only one ship or plank were to cross to Jerusalem,
I would go with it." This marvelous trust in the
goodness of God never failed him. Later amid
persecutions from zealous but imprudent ecclesi-
astics, it would stand him in good stead. How
suited to him are the lines of Tennyson:

"Love took up the harp of Life, and smote on all the
   cords with might;
Smote the cord of Self, that trembling passed in
   music out of sight."

During the trip to Cyprus he narrowly escaped
serious consequences of his love for His Master.
Certain of the crew, reprimanded for their un-
ashamed wicked life, plotted to leave him on an
uninhabited island. The God, Who had other
plans for this apostolic soul, drove the ship off
such a course. Hence in September of 1523, he
reached the goal of his heart's desire, the Holy
Land.

The truly Christ-like soul of Loyola was filled
with holy satisfaction as he set foot in that land
where his God had dwelled in human form. As the
heart of the faithful son kindles with warmth and
pride when it enters the native soil of the father,
so this humble follower of Jesus Christ, felt that

soul nourished by fruitful meditation, almost bursting with joy on touching the earthly Jerusalem. Wrapt in prayer and penance, he journeyed to the spots indicated by well-authenticated tradition as blessed by contact with the Word Made Flesh. Lovingly he lingered where the Precious Blood had been shed and his redemption purchased. So enamoured of the Holy Land did this valiant Saint become that he felt he might well spend his days here in penitential practices. When he broached the matter to the Franciscans in charge of the shrines, it appeared as if he would have this desire. The provincial, however, refused. When the ardent Ignatius offered to accept all dangers, the hasty friar threatened excommunication. No such harshness was needed; the obedient penitent, schooled at Manresa, meekly accepted the decision. The next day he embarked for Europe, which he reached after two months of the severest weather.

The Spanish courtier and cavalier, having completed both his year of prayer at Manresa, and his journey of penance to the Holy Land, was now ready to prepare for his life-work in the service of that King Whom he had discovered while convalescing at Loyola. Ever since he had made the eventful decision he had been considering what form his sacrifice would take. Amid the quiet of Manresa he had practically decided that his contribution to the campaign of Christ would be a company of devoted men who, like light-armed infantry, would be always at the disposal of the Supreme Commander, the Bishop of Rome. Wisdom told him, however, that in the condition of Europe, the only valuable soldier was the trained one. In the ranks of Christ, training meant education. Ignatius then reflected that he was thirty-three years old. Was the struggle too great? The will that had bowed to the sawing of the surgeons at Pamplona and Loyola, that had been strengthened and governed by penance at Manresa, was equal to the proposition now before it. If education was necessary for the battle then the cost was nothing. His mind was on the results. As during the World War, men stepped from civil life into army barracks, there by labor, rigorous discipline, coarse food, arduous exercise, to fit themselves for the battles of Europe, so Ignatius Loyola, Spanish noble, successful soldier, stripped himself of his years with their dignity and entered the classroom to sit beside boys twenty-five years his junior.

This stern resolution forces admiration. Deep must have been the love that brought about such a sacrifice. Men in the world can realize what a humiliation this course meant. Some give their

# ST. IGNATIUS LOYOLA

money to the Master, some even their time and their energy. Ignatius gave himself with his rank and pride. Why is it that he has so few imitators in the world? This step should be a clarion-call to sincere citizens of the Church to do something for her advancement in the present. If he could make such tremendous sacrifices, many should show a little concern for the welfare of religion in the crisis of today. The church and the state need men of this stamp. Religion and civilization should profit by the example humbly given by this nobleman of Spain.

At Barcelona our Saint commenced his educational career. When he had made sufficient progress among the youths, he went to the University at Alcala. While here his desire to win converts for the Master led him to form associations with the other students. From Barcelona four young men who were attracted by his sincerity, had entered the university with him. The efforts Ignatius made through spiritual conferences to win disciples, brought the watchful Spanish Inquisition upon him. Arrested, and tried, he was acquitted of false teaching but ordered to cease such activity until he made a course in theology. This unjust sentence caused him, after consulting the archbishop of Toledo, to leave Alcala, and proceed to the University of Salamanca. Much to his sor-

73

row, he found himself in the same narrow atmosphere. As long as he kept to his books, he had peace. When, however, he sought to aid by his spiritual advice some of the sincere people, who admired this reserved, strong character, he experienced the same treatment. Spain was not the place for unlicensed lecturers. His preaching won for him at Salamanca a worse prison than at Alcala. When some of his followers offered him commiseration, he ardently replied, "There are not enough handcuffs and chains in Salamanca, but that I desire more for the love of God." After much delay, occasioned by the red tape of inquisitors, the innocent man was acquitted, but again warned to cease his activities. The inconsistency of Spain's tribunals begot in this sincere, zealous follower of Christ the ambition to shake the dust of these cities from his feet. With the avenues barred and bolted against him, with the wings of his lofty spirit clipped, he quickly determined that France in place of Spain should be the theatre of his action. It required only a short time to collect his few belongings. Ignatius, the soldier of Jesus, bought a mule, and started for the kingdom of France. Thus it was that the land that had so successfully battled against the Moorish infidels, lost the enviable honor of being the cradle of the Society of Jesus, and France, eldest daughter of the Church of Truth, became the fertile soil, where the seeds nourished at Manresa, now transplanted, produced abundant fruit.

It was on February 2, 1528, that a tired, yet gritty student entered the precincts of Paris, to enroll in its world-famed university. This institution with its schools of theology, medicine, law, as well as arts, had about ten thousand pupils on its register. Although when he left Spain, he was provided with money by some good friends, through his charity to one in distress, he was obliged to take lodgings in a hospital. Anxious not to lose any time, he immediately began his studies. He suffered much from his lack of resources. When summer came, therefore, he took to begging through Belgium and even England in order to be prepared for the following year. He was fortunate in obtaining for assistance in his studies a young man who had just completed the matter, Peter Faber, a Savoyard, about whom much will later be heard.

The earnest scion of Loyola was not in Paris long when his remarkable faculty of drawing others to him, began to act again to his disadvantage. The magnetic personality, which later served him so well in governing thousands of religious scattered over Europe and America, drew about him the curious and noble students who recognized his genius. Some of the professors, whose uninteresting, optional lectures suffered from competition with this uneducated Spaniard, reported him to the authorities. Matters for a while took on a very serious aspect. Ignatius was to be humiliated and then dismissed. In France, however, there was opportunity for truth to be defended. Straightforward, and honorable, Ignatius appealed to the sense of justice in these representatives of authority. Success, therefore, attended his tact. Eventually he was unmolested in his life in Paris. Its university gave him the education he desired as well as the friends who were the nucleus of his company for his King.

From the time when he commenced his education, he was searching for some who would be his allies in the work he had in mind for God. Prayer and reflection had convinced him that the age needed a new organization to cope with the adversaries against whom revealed religion had to contend. It became evident to this disinterested man that as Dominic in the twelfth century had instituted a religious order to meet the conditions of the time, so in this sixteenth century some society, devoted to the Pope, unshackled from any ties of the civil powers, thoroughly fitted by education to instruct the people, must come into existence. While in Spain he seemed to have the first recruits but they did not persevere. Peter Faber, his tutor, proved to be the first subject of value. This young man, devoted to God from his youth, was so beset by scruples, that he was ready to discard his early ambitions of the priesthood. As he grew to admire the solid judgment of the Spaniard, who came to him with such profound humility for assistance in his studies, he opened his soul gradually to him. He was not disappointed. He soon realized that he had a safe guide as well as a noble exemplar. At the suggestion of Ignatius he went through the spiritual exercises and then offered himself as an ally. This Faber would not be the least in the company that would give glory to Christ.

The second catch of the prudent and zealous Ignatius was his best and most famous. There was studying in Paris another Spaniard of noble family who was making a record for scholarship, Francis Xavier. When his fellow-countryman tried to turn his talents to the Church he met only disdain. The Ignatius of old probably remembered that "faint heart ne'er won fair lady." Here was a prize worth perseverance. Loyola would win him by his own coin. Francis had in mind a successful career as a university professor. The wily Saint procured for him pupils. Such good conduct won from Francis admiration and friendship.

# HERALDS OF THE KING

When Ignatius decided that the time was opportune he started to cannonade the strong citadel with the powerful thought of the Master-Strategist: "What doth it profit a man if he gain the whole world and suffer the loss of his own soul? Or what shall a man give in exchange for his soul?" Xavier with his mind crowded with ideas of temporal glory and worldly honors must have acknowledged:

"Yet ever and anon a trumpet sounds
From the hid battlements of eternity."

That call sounded by the saintly Ignatius in the ears of the worldly-minded Francis was not in vain. That thought of eternity placed many times before the reasonable mind of the brilliant professor, coupled with the fervent prayers of Ignatius, gained for Christ his most ardent missionary after St. Paul.

Further success gave confidence to the plans of our Saint. Two young men who had learned in Spain of the capabilities of this fervent student and had followed him to France, were soon persuaded to embrace his cause. When Simon Rodriquez of Portugal, and Bobadilla, another Spaniard, affiliated themselves to him, Ignatius pulsating with enthusiasm, felt that the time was ripe to weld the material into some form, and make his long dream of a society a reality.

Certainly no one present realized what the meeting of those seven men would mean. The plans formed were very general. Some of the company had yet to finish their studies. Ignatius commenced the deliberations with a prayer to the Holy Ghost. All announced their readiness to devote themselves to the service of God and souls. They then decided that they should make three vows, one of poverty, one of chastity, and one of a pilgrimage to the Holy Land at the completion of their studies. After their return they would become priests. With the instinct that Ignatius always manifested towards the Mother of God, the little band gathered at the chapel of St. Denis on the great feast of Mary's Assumption. Peter Faber, the only priest in the group, celebrated Mass during which all pronounced the vows. They also agreed to meet in this chapel on the same feast during the two succeeding years in order to renew their promises. When that time had expired all would have concluded their courses at the university. Such was the simple beginning of what developed into one of the most powerful forces that the world has known. The perfected organization became the salt of the earth. Its sons rejuvenated Christendom and extended its confines to the utmost parts of the world. Great oaks from little acorns grow. On that day, the Feast of Mary's Assumption, 1534, was conceived a society that became the schoolmaster of the noblest minds in Europe, of which the members have grown to over twenty thousand.

Ignatius, whose studies were concluded, was advised to make a trip to his native Spain. His failing health prohibited him from further intensive work at the university. After eleven years of patient fidelity, he had attained the degree of master of arts. The brethren hoped that a sojourn in his own country might restore the vitality shattered from excessive fasting and constant visits to the sick and afflicted. He also had another office to fulfill. He was delegated by some of his confreres to settle their temporal affairs inasmuch as they were bent on renouncing all possessions. While thus seeking his health and acting for others, he did not miss an opportunity to serve his Master. In Spain he gathered about him the children to teach them catechism. He established organizations for the sick and the poor. He urged the men and women to have recourse to the sacraments. Like a true apostle, while thus assisting others he had no care for himself. He refused the offers of his brother to provide him creature comforts and made plans to return to Paris as soon as he had transacted the business affairs of his band.

After a tedious journey across Europe, he reached Venice in January, 1537. Here the six, with three more who had joined them, met him. They had stopped at Rome on their way; there they were graciously received by Pope Paul III who not only granted them permission to make a pilgrimage to the Holy Land, but also gave them alms to assist them. They likewise had obtained from the Holy Father faculties for all to be ordained and to administer the sacraments. At Venice, therefore, they were ordained and all but Ignatius celebrated their first Mass. He out of reverent fear waited almost a year. Because of the hostile Turks it was altogether impossible to fulfill their vow regarding the Holy Land; they accordingly decided that they must do what they had agreed upon as an alternative, that is, place themselves at the disposition of the Pope. Ignatius and two others were selected to confer with the Holy Father, while the rest would preach to the inhabitants of the neighboring cities. When the question at this juncture was proposed, "What answer shall we make if someone asks, who we are?" Ignatius without hesitation replied, "You will reply that you belong to the Company of Jesus; that will be our name." True men of God, they lost no time in using the powers and gifts they had received to make Jesus better known and loved.

While on this journey to the Pope, there occurred a vision which profoundly affected Ignatius. At La Storta, about fifteen miles from Rome, they had entered a little chapel. The Saint, wrapt in prayer, saw the Christ Jesus with the cross on His Shoulder. He looked at Ignatius and said, "I will be propitious to you at Rome." When he related the miracle to his companions the humble man said, "I do not know what will become of us at Rome, perhaps we shall be crucified." The meaning of the Master's words became evident, however, when Pope Paul III bestowed lavish praise upon them for their Christ-like spirit, delegated Lainez to teach in one of the papal universities, and urged the others to conduct the ministry of preaching and the sacraments.

When the disciples of Ignatius saw official favor courting them, and various duties in widely separated places being assigned to them, they felt that it was necessary to decide definitely whether the little, loose organization they had formed was to have any permanent existence or whether they were to perform their ministry as individuals without any bond of unity. Just as they were ready to assemble in conclave an unexpected storm arose to summon all their attention. This was the old enemy, persecution, showing its strength again. A certain faction in Rome, jealous of the popularity and zeal of the brethren, alarmed also because of their readiness to give battle to any unorthodox tenets, thought they saw a chance to crush Ignatius and his companions. Old accusations of heresy were resurrected; new ones, charging hypocrisy, were invented. The hero of Pamplona, who had breasted the squalls of Alcala, Salamanca, and Paris, was agreeable to any fair investigation. He immediately demanded that a judicial trial be instituted, and that the charges be brought into the light of day. His insidious opponents were confounded by this show of courage. They hid, delayed, postponed. Ignatius was no amateur in these matters. He insisted on a verdict from competent authority. His honesty won everyone's approval so that when the Pope, who was absent, returned, he vindicated Ignatius' demand and saw that a decision exonerating the brethren was written.

The increased prestige that came from this trouble made the company realize that the question of their institute had to be solved without delay. Gathered together in Rome, they, after prayer, discussed all phases of the matter. Unanimously they agreed that for the greater glory of

God, Whose work would be best done by the strength coming from mutual encouragement, a permanent religious order must be formed. They also concluded that a superior who would maintain office for life was necessary to keep the members under authority. Their work would be first of all whatever the Pope would demand of them; each member would vow to go any place at the command of the head of the church. Specifically they would exercise the offices of preaching, catechising children, ministering the sacraments, and caring for the sick.

It is needless to remark that the company was almost entirely the work of Ignatius. Whatever offices of zeal the members embraced, were due to his spiritual outlook. He had found these recruits in the world with very shallow ideas of religion. Through wise direction, through spiritual exercises, he had turned their minds to higher things. As Christ was the model for the apostles, he was the living exemplification of the true religious life for the students whom he called from university life. His ministrations to the sick and poor were their book of instruction. His love for the little neglected children was their inspiration. His lofty ideas of devoting his energies to the conversion of the heathen were the fires that inflamed their souls with apostolic zeal. In the offices that we

# ST. IGNATIUS LOYOLA

watch the growth to guide and correct it, so the Spanish cavalier would be the directing genius of the powerful order. As the captain of industry from his office in the big skyscraper is the ultimate reason for the successful business-venture, and must receive the credit for its results, so Ignatius, slaving in the house at Rome, sending out his spiritual soldiers, guiding and encouraging and correcting them by letters constantly written, must be appraised as the successful captain of the glorious organization for the spread and purification of religion.

The drafting of a set of constitutions for this society and an endeavor to obtain a clearer and more generous bull of approval from the Pope, were two tasks that demanded his immediate attention. He appealed to all the professed members for suggestions regarding the constitutions. After many revisions, this work was completed to the satisfaction of all. To elicit a new bull of approval from Rome required much tact. The original had many restrictions and lacked clearness. So successful was he in this regard that the new bull issued by Pope Julius III, is considered as the real basis of the society.

According to this document as well as the first papal approval, one of the duties of the Jesuits would be the conversion of the heathen. We can recall that when the first recruits were resolving upon their future life they decided to go to the Holy Land or to place themselves at the disposition of the Holy Father. Even before the canonical institution of the order, the King of Spain asked for two of the Fathers for the missions in India. Francis Xavier was the only one that Ignatius could spare at the time. His accomplishments in this work are too well known to need narration. He is regarded as the greatest missionary after St. Paul. He labored first in India, then in Japan, and was on his way to China when he died. Other members of the order were sent by Ignatius to labor with him as they were to be had and were needed. The marvelous fruits of this apostolate were the joy of the Christian world. The letters that Xavier wrote to Ignatius narrating his work, describing the difficulties and the successes, were read by all the members of the order, and circulated among the laity for their edification. To Ignatius belongs the credit for the vocation of the man, for selecting him for the start of the society's foreign missionary activity, and for his perseverance amid trying obstacles. Confronted by all manner of trials, he looked to the Father-General for advice and encouragement, and felt refreshed on reading his instructions. The noble bond of brotherhood that held these two men of God together is an example for those in the world as well as those in religion. Ignatius later opened missions in Ethiopia and Brazil, which, while not as successful as that in India, are evidences of the interest of the man in this part of the Church's work. From the days that he had spent in contemplation at Manresa he burned with an irrepressible desire to have Jesus Christ known by all men. As founder and first general of the Jesuit Order, he established as one of its essential duties the preaching of Christianity to the infidel.

Ignatius also grasped thoroughly the necessity of education for those who were to be the guides of the laity. For this reason he endured many sacrifices during his own life. He appreciated full well that as Pope has said,

> " 'Tis education forms the common mind;
> Just as the twig is bent the tree's inclined."

Therefore, when he was forming the rules of the new society, he strictly enjoined that all candidates should be well-trained in the arts and sciences. The best teachers were to be obtained for the novices of the institute. The professed would be prepared to expound scientifically the principles of their religion and to answer all objections to it.

The first colleges founded and conducted by the

cohorts of Ignatius were only for the members of the society. After some years the policy was changed so that seculars were admitted. While Ignatius was not the primary mover in this innovation, it was brought about while he was general and with his approval. He was the one who chose the Fathers for this particular work, arranged the curriculum, and laid down the rules of government. He so directed these colleges that they soon became the equal and later the superior of all other institutions. Whether or not he foresaw the part that this work would take in the society, is irrevelant. To him directly must be given the credit for providing an order of such highly educated religious in every nation in Europe. To him also belongs praise for making the Jesuit colleges the schools for all youths seeking a complete Christian education.

The mighty influence that the son of Loyola exercised in opposing the religious revolutionaries of the sixteenth century is known to all students of history. While it is not true to say that this was the purpose for which he enrolled his spiritual company, it certainly seemed providential that this new force arose to help the suffering church. To offset the diabolical work of the German friar, Luther, of whom it might be said, "Confusion now hath made its masterpiece," Ignatius appeared as

# ST. IGNATIUS LOYOLA

the apostle of light. If this youthful Spanish cavalier had dreamed of being a valiant soldier defending the right, the mature Ignatius, arrayed in the livery of Christ, fulfilled those dreams by collecting and maneuvering a spiritual army to protect and preach the teachings of his Heavenly Father.

The secret of his success and influence was that his religious were instructed in their preaching to be positive exponents of the doctrine of the Church. If others made the mistake of indulging in diatribes, the preachers of Ignatius were to avoid attacking and condemning, and bend their energies to placing in a firm yet courteous manner the teaching of Christ before men. Therefore the Pope chose the Jesuits to occupy chairs in the universities of Rome and to go through all Italy instructing the simple people. In France too, particularly at the University of Paris, the members of the society were a wall of defense against the heretics who flocked thither from Germany and Switzerland. The force that the order became in Germany, the heart of the rebellion, needs hardly be mentioned. Ignatius established at Rome the German College to raise up valiant sons of Germany to defend the true religion in their own country. Peter Faber, one of the original Jesuits, proved to be a Daniel come to judgment against those who were robbing the peasantry of their faith. Brilliant as a preacher, with the zeal of a Stephen, this man of God journeyed everywhere restoring confidence to bishops discouraged at the defections, and recalling the laity to the sacraments. Even more conspicuous than Faber, among those who carried out this program of ministering to the harassed and distressed Germany, was one of the first natives to join the Society of Jesus, Peter Canisius. This noble soul, filled with love for the truth of Christ, became one of the finest preachers of the age. He was in truth a thorn in the side of the reform. While his ability to reach the minds of the simplest made him always in demand, his rapier of keen logic unsettled his adversaries. The assistance which he gave not only to the German bishops but to the Pope, for whom he acted as legate, won for him the attention of the universal church. Along with these intellectual qualities, he had such an appreciation of sanctity that he has recently been officially recognized as one of God's saints. The world will never know in its completeness the debt owed to Ignatius Loyola for his opposition to the enemies of revealed religion in the sixteenth century.

Two means which he insisted upon his brethren constantly inculcating for the upbuilding and rejuvenation of religion in all countries, were the sacraments of Penance and Eucharist. The laity had gradually lost the use of these fecund sources of spiritual life. Their lives were barren as a result. When Ignatius in his early years of conversion had approached Holy Communion once a week, he was regarded as an oddity. When his followers preached this doctrine they were even attacked. He, however, knew the teaching of Christ. He realized the reason for the lack of living faith. He urged his subjects, therefore, to strive always to train the people to make frequent use of the channels of heavenly strength. Due to this wise legislation, these sacraments became again the means of preserving the morals of Europe.

Amid all these diverse labors, Ignatius was enduring poor health which was taking its toll of a constitution weakened by much mortification. From the time of his selection as general he left Rome only once. His time was conscientiously employed in building up the order, establishing it on such a solid basis that it would withstand the ravages of time and the wiles of its enemies. At the same time he was most devoted to his personal sanctification. While his time was the property of all the brethren, he never neglected long hours of meditation. He realized the value of communion with his Master, and constantly sought to add to the store of precious graces he possessed.

To the members who dwelled with him in the Roman house he was a source of sublime edification. Although tending to the needs of the order now scattered throughout Europe, America, India and Japan, he interested himself in the troubles of the humblest brother in the house. To him can be applied the lines that Tennyson wrote of Wellington:

> "Rich in saving common sense,
> And as the greatest only are,
> In his simplicity, sublime."

To those who were sick, Ignatius was an unfailing nurse. Often when all were supposed to be in bed for the night, this kind father would steal into the room of an afflicted religious, to offer comfort. When wrongs had to be righted he would always prove a tactful superior, and a forgiving master. Patient under crosses that came through the inconstancy of former friends, he taught those about him the worth of close intimacy with the Divine Savior.

Thus for sixteen years he labored for the glory of his chosen Master until the weak body could no longer stand the strain. Because he had been sick so often, those in attendance did not realize the

# ST. IGNATIUS LOYOLA

condition of their spiritual father. It was on July 30th, 1556, that he told Father Polanco, who was his helper, that he had not long to live. Always devoted to the vicar of Christ, he asked that the Pope be notified of his serious illness and his blessing obtained. Father Polanco, who consulted the doctor, advised waiting until the morrow. In simple obedience, worthy of the humblest lay-brother, Ignatius bowed in resignation. In the early hours of the following morning, before aid could be summoned even to administer Extreme Unction, the soul of this great warrior of Christ started for its heavenly home to receive its well-earned reward. It was meet that one who lived so humbly should die in the exercise of that same divine virtue.

The life of this friend of God was more than ordinary. The sacrifice that he made to serve his Master, stamped him as a real soldier of Christ. The zeal with which he pursued his vocation was worthy of a saint. The masterful way that he won disciples, trained them in the school of the Savior, united them as brethren in a religious order, proved the firmness of his faith as well as the depth of his practical charity. As Professor Paul van Dyke says so well, "Not simply the form of the Company was from Ignatius; the spirit was

97

also his. No founder of a religious order ever wrote so much to his followers, but the elaborate system of correspondence by which the whole Company was kept in touch with every part of it was only very carefully devised machinery. So long as Ignatius lived and until those who had known him well were mostly gone, the living spirit of him who was to his followers not only the General but 'our Father Ignatius,' animated the entire company, and the feet, the hands, the voices of the missioners and teachers were doing his work." At the time of his death the society had grown to a thousand members, divided into twelve provinces having forty-four colleges. When his company continued to function successfully after his death, and testimonies came from many sources of the fruitful results of his apostolate, the various Popes realized the soundness of the Christian character of the founder, Ignatius. Pope Paul V, therefore, beatified him in 1609, and Gregory XV, in 1622, declared him a saint of God.

Although dead now these many years the soul of St. Ignatius Loyola still "goes marching on." Thousands today are following in his footsteps. Loyal men in the world are regularly making in religious houses retreats which he instituted. Religious men and women are inspired to emulate his unworldliness, and to consecrate themselves completely and irrevocably to the same Master. To all who have read his life, and admire his heroic ideals, his love for the instruction of little children, his appreciation of education, his zeal for the frequent use of the sacraments, St. Ignatius exclaims, "Go, thou, and do likewise."

# St. Teresa of Avila

THESE BEAUTIFUL lines of Joyce Kilmer,

"O bleeding feet, with peace and glory shod!
O happy moth, that flew into Sun!"

may appropriately be addressed to Teresa of
Avila, the Spanish mystic, authoress, foundress,
and saint of the sixteenth century. It is unques-
tionable that she is among the greatest women
that ever lived. Her experience with life awakens
the interest of men and women of all classes and
creeds. In an age when her sex is commonly supposed to have been in the far background, she was
a conspicuous reformer of age-long abuses and the
leader of men. Her valiant battle in conquering
self, her successful efforts to better her times, her
sublime conduct amid serpentine persecution are a
sermon to heroic characters. Her single-minded-
ness while consorting with those in highest society,
her faithful strivings after union with God, prove
her an inspiration to all ambitious souls. Her interest in affairs of advantage to mankind, and her
indifference to hampering traditions win for her
the attention of pioneering souls today. Her ability to cope with opposition, her prudent handling

# ST. TERESA OF AVILA

of men, her tact in governing women, mark her with the stamp of genius. Her prolific writings, embodying the frank story of her personal pursuit of virtue, her arduous struggles for deep sanctity, the intimate union of her soul with God, as well as her encounters with the lay and ecclesiastical powers that were too conservative for her progressive ideas, are mines of practical advice for people of all ages and walks of life. In a critical time when the social position of woman is undergoing many changes, when the country of Spain is in a state of unrest, it should be immensely interesting to observe the life and accomplishments of this feminine saint of Spain in the dynamic sixteenth century.

It was in the year that the ambitious but infamous Thomas Wolsey received the red hat of the cardinalate from Pope Leo X and just three years before Martin Luther paved the way for the Protestant Revolution by nailing his ninety-five theses to the door of the University-Church of Wittenburg, that Teresa de Ahumada first saw the light of day. In a house where there were already five boys and three girls, this daughter to Alonzo and Beatrice, his second wife, arrived on March 28, 1515. The family was of noble blood, and had inhabited the town of Avila for many centuries. This Avila had won for itself an enviable place in Spanish history because of its constant heroic struggles against the bloodthirsty Moors, who had unceasingly filled it with terror. The youth quickly learned the tales of those valiant exploits of its ancestors and drank in their noble courage. The little girl Teresa, having practical Catholic parents, also understood from the lives of the saints, how the martyrs of God by their sacrificial deaths, won everlasting happiness. Her active mind asked, "Why could not she be captured now as a Christian in the territory of the Saracens, and by martyrdom purchase speedily the kingdom of heaven?" By such an oblation she planned to obtain readily her soul's salvation. With these convictions, she persuaded her brother Rodrigo, three years her senior, to set out with her for the territory still held by the Moors. Fortunately for the good father and mother, and also for posterity, which would reap cherished fruits from the example of this same Teresa, an uncle met the adventurers and led them back to the homestead. This escapade is important in that it provides the key to the inner life of the Saint. She was dominated always by one passion; the attainment of heavenly glory. No sacrifice was too great to purchase it, no battles too ardent to ensure it. With her growth and development, it will be more pronounced and assertive. Later she will thus express this philosophy: "Remember that you have but one soul, that you can die but once, that you have but one short life; that there is but one glory, and this is eternal, and you will endure many things." What a boon it would be to society if all the young received this teaching in a satisfactory way. What a need there is of inculcating this conviction in every school of education. Such realization of one's dependence upon God, and one's creation for a future unending life, would be the salvation of a civilization that is hanging in the balance. Never so much as at present has there been the imperative necessity for individuals to be conscious of their responsibility to Almighty God, and of so ordering and restraining their moral actions as to keep themselves always ready for entrance into heavenly glory.

The early and unexpected death of Dona Beatrice, loving and gentle mother of Teresa, led to a crisis in the well-ordered home. She was an excellent type of the Spanish lady of the time, devoted to her children, seeking always her happiness in the family gathered about her. When she was only thirty-three and Teresa fourteen, God summoned her to her lasting home. The blow was severely felt by the household, particularly by the emotional and devoted Teresa. She had made a companion of the good mother. The

103

child's deep faith, however, immediately came to the surface. She relates that when this grave, heart-rending misfortune befell her, she hastened to the little shrine of the Virgin Mary that was part of that Christian home. With her eyes suffused with tears, she dropped on her knees before the image of Mary Immaculate, and sobbingly told the Mother of God that henceforth she must be her mother. Looking now at the life of the Saint, one can perceive how well Mary responded to the simple plea of the motherless girl. Such filial devotion to the Mother of God produced one of the Church's highest and also most practical saints. The Queen of Heaven sustained this adopted daughter amid many temptations and unusual crosses, and guided her safely to her destined place in this world, and later to her earthly mother in heaven. This brings to mind St. Bernard's words, "No one ever had recourse to thy protection, O Mary, without obtaining relief." This incident in the early life of St. Teresa should deeply impress all with the value of being strongly attached to the Mother of God. Every lover of goodness should clasp Mary Immaculate to his soul with hoops of steel.

The home deprived of Dona Beatrice was like a castle without a guarding door; it was open to all influences. The older brothers, fired with the

# ST. TERESA OF AVILA

glowing stories of the new world of America, left for there to seek their fortunes. Mary, stepchild of Dona Beatrice, the oldest of the children, naturally assumed the place of a mother. Unfortunately, there were so many differences in the natures of Mary and Teresa that it was nigh unto impossible for them to be close to one another. The latter, keen, active, emotional, loved to read the romantic novels which her mother had constantly for diversion amid her trying duties. This comely girl also became a favorite with some cousins who often visited the home. One of these boys showed a particular affection which she reciprocated in all innocence. A spinster relative whom Dona Beatrice never liked, encouraged the maiden in this flirtation. It was entirely harmless but won the speedy censure of the stern Alonzo when he perceived it. He, without further reflection, decided that this motherless daughter would be better guarded in some convent-school. Summarily he arranged for the boarding of his fourteen-year-old girl among the sisters of the Augustinian order in the Convent of Our Lady of Grace.

Life here was not as unpleasant as it first appeared. The maiden was mortally humiliated by the turn affairs had taken. She also exaggerated in her mind the episode with her cousin. If she had been imprudent, however, she had done nothing at all reprehensible. The sensible confessor soon reassured her. To help matters, she found a sweet calm and content among the sisters that had been lacking since her gentle mother had passed away. She enjoyed her little tasks, and became attached to the various spiritual exercises in which the boarders were allowed to take part. One of the sisters took a special interest in her and won her confidence. Teresa, withal, had no intention of following in the footsteps of the pious woman. Her future course was still a great mystery to her. The one thing she was resolved upon was to save her immortal soul. This was the only conviction she had; the spirit that manifested itself when she ran away to be a martyr among the Moors, was still dominant. Life might have its complexities but there was only one goal worth striving for. While she was peacefully participating in the curriculum of the convent and enjoying frequent chats with Sister Maria, she was taken sick. When the trouble defied ordinary diagnosis, Alonzo was summoned. Filled with grief, he took his precious daughter home to obtain the best medical attendance.

This period, which commenced with her return to the family-castle, had many vicissitudes which led finally to Teresa finding her true self. It was decided that she might improve at the home of Mary, who was now comfortably married. While on the way, she stopped at the house of a brother of her father. This uncle had become a religious after his wife died. He devoted all his days to spiritual works. Teresa, weakened by the strange malady, had no inclination to engage in deep religious discourses. With her usual good nature, to please the old man, she consented, however, to read to him each day. Naturally many of the thoughts from the book remained in her mind. After her brief stay, she passed on to her sister's where the peace and care procured for her gradually a return to health. When the anxious father saw this happy turn of affairs with his comely Teresa, now no longer a child, he bade her to accompany him to the Ahumada castle.

As mistress here, Teresa enjoyed much happiness until she definitely decided what was the will of God in her regard. Her stay at home lasted about four years. She proved a good mistress for Alonzo who needed some one to manage his household. She also had many courtiers who begged her father for her hand. He, however, wanted the devotion of this faithful maiden; she with consummate wisdom, was not making any hasty judgments. The spiritual reading she had engaged in to satisfy her uncle, had given to her many serious thoughts. During these days while caring for the home, she had opportunity to reflect upon the meaning and the value of life. She had the solid conviction that:

> "Virtue alone outbuilds the Pyramids,
> Her monuments shall last when Egypt's fall."

She plainly realized that nothing must separate her from the kingdom of heaven. She also felt that whatever would guarantee her that pearl of great price was what was to be followed. Prayer in solitude exercised a powerful influence during these days of indecision. She fortunately happened upon the conversion of St. Augustine whose dedication to God impressed her indelibly. She thought of her mother's life, of her own days of temptation, of the year and a half spent in the convent. Only those who have gone through this milling can understand the mental agony that the maiden endured before coming to a final conclusion. Mature deliberation, punctuated by prayer, led to a decision; God would be her only aim and ambition in this life that she might be sure of Him in the endless one to come. Although just out of her teens, she not only believed but appreciated keenly that:

# ST. TERESA OF AVILA

"Life is a highway and its milestones are the years,
And now and then there's a toll-gate where you
     buy your way with tears,
It's a rough road and steep road and it stretches
     broad and far,
But at last it leads to a golden Town where golden
     houses are."                    *(Kilmer)*

In order to carry out her resolution she decided
to manifest her mind to her father. She knew that
her strong natural pride would force her to fulfill
what she told another was her purpose.

All the strength of character that Teresa possessed had to be drawn upon to persevere in her
decision. Her father cried loudly against any such
course. Time enough for that when he was dead
and gone. Her duty now was to offer him comfort
and consolation. She was to be the staff of his
declining years when old age rested its harsh, un-
welcome hand upon him. The daughter had prepared for all this. Only after considering justly
the rights of all had she made her decision. If she
were needed at home she would not have spoken
of her vocation. Her spiritual welfare was at
stake. Future events ratified her conclusion. To
one of her brothers she again looked for assistance through example. As Rodrigo years ago
offered to seek martyrdom with her, so at this
crisis Antonio decided to enter the Dominicans
when his Teresa would start for Carmel. To this

order she was attracted by a friend who had already joined it. She tells in her autobiography that she would have entered any other order so long as she could have cared for her soul; "I thought more of the salvation of my soul now, and made no account of my own ease." In 1535,—Teresa was now twenty years old,—the brother and sister left the home of their earthly father to enter that of their Heavenly One. Alonzo, unable to change the mind of his much-loved daughter, generously went at the proper time to arrange the temporal part of the contract. In the convent of the Incarnation, of the Order of Carmel, in Avila, Teresa, through God's grace and her determined will-power began her religious life.

The contentment she found at Our Lady of Grace, which passed when she left there through sickness, returned within the walls of the Incarnation. She gave her heart to the Master unselfishly; He generously filled it with love. While difficulties presented themselves, she saw in all the provident will of her Heavenly Father. Some of the community envied the spirit of devotion of this new postulant; some even imputed to her false motives. Teresa, nevertheless, firm in faith, sought her peace in God, and tranquilly pursued her chosen way. What did unfortunately interfere seriously with this happy and self-immolating

# ST. TERESA OF AVILA

service of God was another attack of that strange malady which had forced her father to withdraw her from the convent of Our Lady of Grace. This recurrence became so serious, and so baffling to the doctors called, that the Superior allowed the anxious Alonzo to remove his daughter for the time from the convent in the hope that some treatment might be found to restore her to health.

This trial was to be a source of much physical suffering for Teresa. She accepted it with a patience that was admirable. When the local doctors made no progress, her devoted father decided to take her to a woman who had the ɩ putation of accomplishing extraordinary cures through her knowledge of various herbs. Since the medicine proposed could not be had until the spring, Teresa was to remain again with her stepsister, Mary. The aged uncle, who had received such happiness from his niece's other visit, insisted that the sick nun must pause once more at his home. In the providence of God, this charity on the part of the suffering Teresa brought rich rewards. The spiritual ideas that this meditating recluse broached to the girl, the mortified life that he led, the religious books that he had Teresa read to him, all left an indelible mark upon the active, impressionable, intelligent soul. Through his example and influence, she made rapid progress in interior prayer. Her trying sickness afforded the necessary solitude for this practice. Turning her soul to God in the midst of her affliction, she made at this time the beginning of that mystical life that was to develop into her later heroic sanctity. Through this relative unconsciously were planted the seeds that were to sprout and flower not only for Teresa Ahumada but also for many who would be attracted by her sincere life and influenced by her prolific idealistic writings.

The result of her visit to the healer indicates the working of the providence of God. So severe were the treatments, and so futile, that the unfortunate subject was more dead than alive when her father removed her. Because of her weakened state, she fell into a trance which those about her took to be death. The mortuary candles were lit about her and the grave in the cemetery of the convent was opened to receive her. Only the insistence of the devoted and grief-stricken father prevented her being buried alive. After four days of coma, Teresa awoke and demanded to be carried back to her monastery. She had left it only to be cured; since the doctors had accomplished nothing, she desired to be in the house of God where she belonged.

Back in the Incarnation, she determined to entrust herself entirely to prayer, particularly to

## ST. TERESA OF AVILA

St. Joseph, who, she felt, was neglected, when he had great power before God. Patiently and confidently, therefore, she sought the assistance of the foster-father of Our Lord. She told herself that he who had been so faithful in God's service, who had played such an important part in the sublime mystery of the Incarnation, could certainly obtain extraordinary favors for his clients. This simple, boundless confidence was not misplaced; St. Joseph proved his fidelity and his influence. What no doctor had been able to bring about, was secured by humble, trusting prayer to St. Joseph. The stricken nun arose from the bed where she had lain, and took her place in the community. Her sisters, who had seen her at the vestibule of death, who regarded her as a hopeless case, marvelled to see her in attendance at the religious exercises. Teresa, happy to be able to resume her chosen life, did not forget him to whom she owed this miraculous recovery. Henceforth she was a persistent advocate of devotion to the foster-father of Christ. She urged all to venerate this saint who had been so close to the Infant Jesus. That her gratitude was not ephemeral is evident from the fact that the first convent she founded was placed under the patronage of St. Joseph, and that all her spiritual children have been ardent apostles of devotion to this Saint. To her also is owed the increased veneration of St. Joseph in the succeeding centuries. Certainly the Christian can copy St. Teresa in this regard. The Virtues of St. Joseph, particularly his self-control amid many trials, should be emphasized. He is a shining example of humble acceptance of the will of Almighty God. As he helped this Saint when all earthly remedies failed, so he will ever listen to his persevering clients, accomplish their wishes, bless their lives, and direct them to the salutary service of the Master.

Teresa followed conscientiously all the rules of the monastery as soon as she had received her strength. Unfortunately the customs of the time were not favorable to the close union of the soul with God. Visitors were welcome at the convents at all hours. When the routine-duties were finished, the nuns were at liberty to go to the parlors. The latter were generally thronged with gossiping, admiring relatives and friends ready to narrate all the big and little happenings in the city. While there could be nothing reprehensible in the practice, surely it was not conducive to sanctity. The distractions of the world quickly found their way into the house of God. As Cardinal Gasquet has said so well, "As rust prevents the attraction of the magnet for iron exercising its natural power, so does dust,—the dust of human conversation,—interfere between our souls and His Almighty drawing of them to Himself. 'Fascinatio nugacitatis obscurat bonum, et inconstantia concupiscentiae transverit sensum sine malitia,'—the bewitching attraction of trifles obscures the good, and the fickleness of concupiscence turns aside the innocent mind." The unfortunate effect this mingling with the world and its votaries had upon this devoted Child of God was to lead her to decide that she was not honorable in seeking and cultivating interior conversation with her Master while taking part in idle talk with lay-visitors. In the conflict between her own practice and the attitude accepted by the community, she allowed the habit of mental prayer to lapse. While she saw the opportunities for precious mystical intercourse with the Savior, she did not see that it was her duty to be different from the rest of the monastery. God in His own good time would enlighten her as to His wishes. She was destined to be His instrument to rid cloistered life of this plague. Through her response to Him when He would unfold the right, she would become the sun that would warm, lighten, and fructify the lukewarm religious spirit of Spain in the sixteenth century.

It was through the sickness of her father that God deigned to touch the conscience of this child of His, and draw her to a closer union with Himself. To the Franciscan confessor ministering to the old man, Teresa explained her difficulty. The keen director of souls had the opportunity to show the nun her duty to foster mystical prayer. Because the Superior at the Incarnation permitted the daughter to remain at home to solace the father in his fatal sickness, Teresa had abundant time to reflect upon the advice of the Franciscan and to put it into practice. Through this heavy cross of her father's suffering and death, the Good God communicated to her precious graces which she accepted. She returned to her former method of silent communing with the Savior, and assiduously persevered in it when she again entered the convent.

This obedience to the voice of God as revealed through the confessor of her father, won from the Master still more valuable graces. The little book given to her by the aged uncle proved to be a veritable mine of spirituality. It gave up to Teresa the nuggets of intimate union with the Sovereign Creator. God communed with His subject in response to her efforts to come to a deeper and more perfect oneness with His Divine Will. What agitated the sincere nun was her inability to obtain a confessor who understood her. Because of the special graces God showered upon her, she mistrusted her own judgment. Different priests to whom she

unbosomed her soul, lacked the spiritual insight to
see the working of God in this extraordinary case.
This predicament resulted in much mental anguish
for her. Providentially that same humble trust in
her Master, which she evinced in early life, protected her in these crises, and enabled her to
ascend the difficult and treacherous inclines of
higher sanctity. Despite the mistakes of some who
belittled her mystical favors, of jealous and gossiping religious who threatened her, and even
sought to have the Inquisition condemn her, she
persevered in her endeavor to renounce herself
and follow in simplicity the commands of the
Savior. God, as a result, preserved His creature
from pitfalls and the snares set by enemies, and
admitted her gradually to the very heights of real
mystical union enjoyed only by His chosen souls.

A truly remarkable and precious evidence of
favor with God came when Our Lord appeared to
her and solved the vexing problem that had been
with her since she entered the convent. Many
times she hesitated as to the will of heaven regarding the periods spent in the convent-parlor. It
was not wrong, but it did not seem right. It looked
like divided allegiance. Her fidelity to prayer was
to win an answer. One day while absorbed in devotion, she saw the Christ before her and heard
from Him these words, "I will not have thee con-

verse with men but with angels." This was the "ipse dixit" that her noble soul needed. Henceforth there would be no vacillating in the attitude of this chosen creature. It was in the year 1558 that Teresa of Ahumada became entirely and forever Teresa of Jesus.

This decisive happening, an extraordinary grace from Almighty God, would be a precious remembrance for the rest of Teresa's days. She recognized it as the answer to many prayers. Moreover, she had reached that stage of self-immolation where to know the will of God was to embrace it. Many new and unusual trials were ordained for this creature. Persecutions from well-meaning religious who should help her, and from laymen who should not have hindered her, will beset her path, and fill it with briars and thorns. These will never deter her: she will always be able to say, "If God is with me, who is against me?" Her deep faith in Jesus will draw strength from the thought that

> "Lo, comfort blooms on pain, and peace on strife,
>     And gain on loss.
> What is the key to Everlasting Life?
>     A blood-stained Cross."

When the Divine Master saw Teresa's acceptance of His manifested Will, He unfolded the great plan that He had destined for her in this world. Often she had lamented the spirit of laxity and worldliness that had crept into the cloistered orders; she had even hoped that the day would come when they would return to their pristine spirit. Little did she realize that in the mind of God this task, delicate and laborious, was to fall upon her shoulders. Her cousin Dona Guiomar and another friend were discussing this situation. The former suggested that they could form a community that would put into practice the severe discipline of the early religious. Teresa was immediately on fire with enthusiasm; it seemed as if she had been waiting for such a spark to enkindle her soul to a burning flame of activity. She exhorted the others to carry out the idea; she told of the good that would result for all sincere religious. The effect was that the matter was settled: they would undertake the establishment of a Carmelite monastery that would be built on rigid mortification and whole-hearted union with Almighty God.

The accomplishment of this bold, and seemingly rash, project was no ordinary task. When Teresa started to mention plans for the building, the obtaining of money, the choosing of the site, the others lost their enthusiasm. The Saint, however, seeking only the glory of God, convinced that this task was His Will, was determined to persevere. Her whole life had been a series of crosses; another could be borne with the help of Him Who feedeth the birds of the air and the fishes of the sea. No doubt she kept repeating to herself those powerful words of the great apostle, St. Paul, "I can do all things in Him Who strengtheneth me." As he endured persecutions of all kinds in his efforts to build up the kingdom of the Savior, Teresa was ready to emulate him. Her fine, practical common sense told her that much fundamental even unpleasant labor was necessary —"Unless the grain of wheat, falling into the ground dieth, it bringeth forth no fruit." Knotted and ugly roots hidden in the soil are far different in appearance from branches and flowers that are gladsome to the eye and the heart; without those ugly roots, however, there could be no lovely fruits and blossoms. She took upon herself the un-welcome task of gathering money for the initial work. She personally superintended the laying of the foundation. Her confessor, a good but timor-ous soul, had allowed her to undertake the project. When opposition raised its mean head, when the religious of Avila voiced their jealousy, the gentle, fearful, confessor lost his courage. He bade the Saint to desist. He feared the flames of hatred that burst forth from those who should have re-joiced that a noble work for the good of religion was in progress. He urged that she wait six months before commencing operations. Teresa, as always, obedient, bowed her head in resignation. If this idea was the will of God all the powers of earth and hell would not be able to frustrate it.

The prudent nun employed the six months in gaining new and stronger allies, whose backing and prestige would insure the success of her plans. If she had the simplicity of the dove, she had also the wisdom of the serpent. The Dominicans, it was evident, were the influential religious of the time in Avila. One, in particular, Father Pedro Ibanez, was regarded as the oracle of orthodoxy. She would win this learned man to the cause so dear to her heart. Her frank sincere manner dispelled what prejudices he had inherited from unthinking critics. Her keen, intelligent presentation of the urgent need of such a religious institute as she outlined made him an easy prey. He saw that the good of the individual souls as well as the condition of the times demanded houses of religion where those desiring to practice perfection would be unhampered by any inroads of the worldly spirit. The effect that his alliance had on the multitude was tremendous. Fickle, indeed, is the popular mind. The timid confessor was now willing to permit his penitent to try her success with the powers of Avila. The zealous and clever nun who had obtained the approval of the bishop by placing the projected monastery under his direction, recommenced her building. Like a gift from heaven was some money from her brother Lorenzo who was piling up some of the gold in America. The populace, having observed the interest and support of the talented preacher, Father Pedro Ibanez, no longer showed its teeth. Gradually, therefore, the Saint saw her ambition becoming a reality. Her iron will was to reap its reward. Although wanting in many things, the house was finally ready for the entrance of Teresa and her first novices. On St. Bartholomew's Day in the year 1562, these radiant enthusiasts gathered in their poverty-stricken chapel for the offering of the first Mass in this newest home of the Master. Out of gratitude for many precious and signal favors, especially for the strength given to her to persevere in her trying labors for Almighty God, St. Teresa called this holy house, destined to be the parent of many others, the Monastery of St. Joseph.

The deep faith displayed by this humble nun in the face of such bitter and malignant persecution proclaims her one of God's greatest saints. Only this trust in heaven enabled her to continue the task placed upon her by the Savior. Lesser souls would have succumbed to the fierce criticism. They

ST. TERESA OF AVILA

would have withered under the scathing innuendoes of short-sighted religious in high places.
Teresa, with all her well-grounded humility took
literally the words of Christ, "Have the faith of
God. Amen, I say to you, that whosoever shall say
to this mountain, be thou removed and be cast into
the sea, and shall not stagger in his heart, but
believe that whatsoever he saith shall be done; it
shall be done unto him." (Mark 11/22-23). Her
days of trial are not over; the flames of opposition
will again break forth. The same God, however,
will be her support and refuge. She will be fortified by the thought, "This is the victory which
overcometh the world, our faith." Glorious would
it be for the Church of God if all Christians, especially those consecrated to the Master, had such
solid and practical realization of the principles of
religion that animated Teresa. Verily the world
would see again a resurrection of the early successes of the gospel, and an evidence of virtue that
would cleanse and purify all society.

At the monastery of St. Joseph Teresa passed
the five happiest years of her life. Chosen superior
against her will, she so conducted the community
that all made progress in the service of God. Her
own humility was an inspiration to the rest. She
insisted in taking her turn at all the tasks of the
household. She was the first to rise in the morn-

ing, and the most earnest in the spiritual exercises. Her wise rule brought peace to the sisters, who accepted cheerfully the rigorous exactions of the severe rule. The practical advice which she gave to these subjects could with immense profit be followed by every one, "Let your desire be to see God, your fear that you may lose Him, your sorrow be in His absence, your joy in all that may draw you to Him; with this guide you will live in much peace." Her tender solicitude for those troubled, her regard for the sick, her efforts to lead all by gentle ways along the rough path of mortification, imbued the new community with her own zeal for the cause of the Master, and led them to rival one another in the pursuit of Christ-like self-denial and sanctity. Such true wisdom and charity are an inspiration to all Christians. If the same desire to assist others, to please God, to advance in holiness, actuated each individual, the vexing problems of life would be easier and more happily solved. From the spirit of joy that circulated through this first foundation of Teresa, it was evident that the approval of Almighty God was upon this work.

The visit of the superior-general of the Carmelite Order to Spain was to break this spell of external peace, start the Saint on a path of fresh activity, and increase the glory of God in her country. By command of the Pope he was making his visitation of all monasteries. The prudent Teresa did not wait for him to appear; she sent him an invitation. His heart was gladdened at the contemplation of this latest Carmelite establishment. The spirit of otherworldliness that dominated it, the peace that prevailed among the religious, the love for poverty, all captivated this man accustomed to receiving complaints and correcting abuses. No doubt, he realized the inspired wisdom of this superior, who in justifying the concept of unadulterated poverty, said, "Poverty is a strong wall. It is a wealth which includes all the wealth of the world; it is complete possession and dominion. What are kings and lords to me if I do not envy them their riches, nor seek to please them, if by so doing I should in the least displease God? What care I for honors, if I know that the honor of a poor man lies in being poor? It seems to me that honors and riches nearly always go together; he who covets honors never hates riches, while he who hates riches seeks no honors.—True poverty, undertaken for the sake of God, bears with it a certain dignity, in that he who professes it need seek to please no one but Him, and there is no doubt that the man who asks no help has many friends.—If poverty is real, it guards purity and all the other virtues better than fine buildings." At any rate, Teresa was so sure that he was charmed by the spirit of this new Carmel that she asked if she might have his permission to institute other houses under the same régime. Rubeo put his seal upon the work of the Saint by granting her his authority to found not only monasteries of women but also two of men.

This favor from the head of all the Carmelites meant the crossing of the Rubicon for St. Teresa. God had chosen and moulded her for great things. The rest of her days would be spent advancing the standard of her Lord by laboring to build new fortresses of prayer and sacrifice. She had already decided that Medina del Campo would be her next site. Commencing that monastery, she bade adieu to all peace and tranquillity. Many times she would look back to the five happy years at her lovely St. Joseph's of Avila. Crowns and kingdoms, however, are won not in castles but on the open field of battle. Teresa will accept generously the manifest will of God. Her noble soul, purified by sacrifice and suffering from the dross of this world, will obtain strength and perseverance from the example of her Model, Who said, "My meat is to do the will of Him Who sent Me." At the time of life when others are casting aside responsibilities and hardships, she will begin a series of journeys that will take her all over Spain. She will

contend with the powers of this world and the
demons of darkness. Altogether she will establish
eighteen monasteries of women and two of men.
She will awaken new religious life in her country.
She will purify and elevate every place that she
visits. Within her monasteries souls, snatched
from the world, will by a life of self-immolation
make atonement for the evils of the age, and by
their quiet unostentatious example, bring to the
minds of men the necessity of seeking always first
the kingdom of God.

Such great accomplishments were not gained
without much suffering on the part of this faithful
servant of God. Her health never ceased to bother
her. At times she appeared to her devoted assist-
ants more dead than alive. Certainly her prayer,
which is the key to her extraordinary life, "Lord,
to suffer or to die," was answered. On different
occasions she arose from a sick bed to found a
new monastery. Her unflagging perseverance amid
such a trial was a constant sermon to her spiritual
daughters. She had written, "To make one step
in the propagation of the faith, and to give one
ray of light to heretics, I would forfeit a thousand
kingdoms." They observed that the sickness that
had caused her such pain in her early days, returned and became aggravated when she was har-
rowed by worry and exposure to every kind

of weather. Such patience under physical weakness, such refusal to be conquered by the ills of the body, won for this devoted servant fresh tokens of love from her Master. Amid all her labors she never ceased to make spiritual progress in the enclosed garden of her own soul. Assuredly that indomitable spirit of Teresa of Jesus will fire new souls to labor more valiantly in the path of difficulties, and to accept religiously crosses sent by heaven.

Burdensome as was this physical trouble, it was the lesser of the crosses given to the Saint. Gold must be tried by fire, and the soul of the disciple of Christ in the furnace of tribulation. The obstacles placed by human hands to the work of Teresa would have disarmed and brought to the ground another soldier.

She had abundant opportunity to exclaim,

"Thank God for the mighty tide of fears
Against me always hurled!
Thank God for the bitter and ceaseless strife
And the sting of His chastening rod."
*(Kilmer)*

The demon of jealousy stalked abroad to thwart the efforts of this chosen soul to restore religion to its pristine spirit of self-immolation and sanctity. The Mitigated Carmelites, as the original monasteries came to be called, felt the new rule a reflection upon themselves and violently opposed it. Other established orders joined in this effort to stamp out the reform of Teresa. The Inquisition was dragged into the controversy and it proceeded to examine minutely the life and writings of the Saint. With her characteristic obedience, Teresa revealed to those zealous investigators the story of her interior and exterior life. The result was that this club of her enemies became powerless. Another source of trouble, that did bring dire anguish and threatened destruction to the convents of Teresa, was the governing coterie of the original order at Rome. Legates came who caused great worry and much sorrow to the souls allied with the new monasteries. Teresa was obliged for a period to cease altogether any active work, and even to fear bodily persecution. Amid all these dangers, however, she never lost her trust in heaven. Her spirit always was, "If God is with me, who is against me?" To her soul she would say:

> "Let nothing trouble thee;
>     Let nothing frighten thee;
> All things pass away;
>     God never changes;
> Patience obtains all things;
>     Who hath God wanteth nothing;
> God alone suffices."

Her faith was rewarded; she saw her enemies lose their strength while she was enabled once more to take up her task of founding new houses where God would be glorified and souls sanctified.

Her unflagging zeal in the service of her Master led her to employ the time when she was hindered from active labors in adding to her writings. Her accomplishments with the pen have won praise from all sources. Not only her own generation but every succeeding one has profited by her works. The story of her life, written at the command of her confessor, is replete with solid wisdom for souls in the world as well as in the cloister. "The Interior Castle" is a mine of spirituality. "The Way of Perfection" has been a guide to many saints. These masterpieces have attracted and drawn fulsome praise not only from her coreligionists but from many outside the pale of the Catholic Church. They offer unimpeachable evidence of the profound common sense of the authoress as well as of her deep spirituality.

As a mark of heaven's approval on her life, Teresa had the friendship of a host of God's chosen souls. St. John of God, that ethereal being whose soul was already in heaven while his body was on earth, was inspired by the delicate love of our Saint for the Savior. Without doubt his prayers were a powerful aid to her reform.

# ST. TERESA OF AVILA

St. Francis Borgia, converted worldling, follower of the great Loyola, manifested his regard by the very practical assistance he gave to Teresa. He recognized the hand of God in her efforts and valiantly defended her against the tongues of her accusers. St. Peter of Alcantara was another of God's elect who put his seal upon this devoted servant of Christ. Through these and other saintly souls, God revealed His love for His humble Teresa and the interest He had in her undertakings.

Encouraged by such stalwart servants of the Almighty, aided visibly by her Savior, Teresa of Jesus tirelessly pursued the road mapped out for her by the providence of God until her never strong body could stand the strain no longer. Like Ulysses, even in her late years she labored valiantly,

> "strong in will
> To strive, to seek, to find, and not to yield."

She was engaged in establishing a new foundation when, worn out from traveling in all kinds of places and weather, she broke under the effort. Those about her urged her to permit an assistant to take the assignment, but her personal attention was insisted upon by those providing the opportunity. After passing over roads practically impassable because of the wet season, she reached the city of Burgos and accomplished her purpose. The populace turned out in mass to honor her, even seeking parts of her habit as relics of a saint. Teresa cared for none of this, although it was a welcome change from what she had been experiencing. She longed only to return to her first love, St. Joseph's of Avila. The will of God, however, did not grant to His servant this consolation. She reached the monastery at Alba de Tormes where she passed the night. Her indomitable spirit enabled her to rise in the morning and make the customary inspection of the house. This was the finish of her work. The Good God, grateful for her generous spirit, had a better and a happier home for her, to which He now took her. On the feast of the great St. Francis of Assisi, the lover of Lady Poverty, in the year 1582, Teresa of Ahumada become Teresa of Jesus, completed her earthly days, and was born into the kingdom of life. Only forty years later, *i.e.* in 1622, she was declared a saint of the Church by Pope Gregory XV.

The spirit that actuated this chosen soul is sorely needed everywhere among Christians. Her realization that only the future life is important should come home to a world in throes of agony and distress because it is immersed in material thoughts. Her devotion to the One and Only God should be an incentive and an inspiration to both laity and religious. Well did the poet Robert Southey write,

> "What will not woman, gentle woman dare,
> When strong affection stirs her spirit up?"

Her accomplishments, due to her constant union with God through prayer, should awaken in the modern representatives of her sex, a desire to emulate her. Her tireless efforts to advance the cause of truth, to bring to the world a knowledge of its duties to the Supreme Intelligence, should inspire all who yearn for a resurrection of Christian principles to enlist in a holy crusade to aid stricken humanity. "Teresa of Jesus, mystic, writer, and saint, apostle of charity, enkindle in the hearts of men today, the fire of love that radiated from your noble heart."

# St. Jane Frances de Chantal

How WELL does Tennyson in one of his lyrics, portray the supernatural attraction of St. Jane Frances de Chantal for Jesus Christ when he has a lover exclaim,

> "My whole soul waiting silently,
> All naked in a sultry sky,
> Droops blinded with his shining eye;
> I will possess him or will die.
>   I will grow round him in his place,
>   Grow, live, die looking on his face.
>   Die, dying, clasp'd in his embrace."

What makes the life of this unusual woman interesting and absorbing is that she was a woman of the world, a wife, a mother, a widow, before becoming a cloistered religious. Here is no recluse who buried herself in youth in a convent, but a being who moved in the royal society of France in the seventeenth century, who tasted its pleasures, and added to its charms. Jane the Saint was a comely maiden, an intensely devoted wife, and a faithful mother before entering religion. She served God as dutifully in the world amid the snares and temptations of French society, as in the Visitation Order. She was an ideal wife, passionately attached to her husband, while striving

## ST. JANE FRANCES DE CHANTAL

in an heroic way to fulfill the counsels of perfection. She stands out conspicuously as a model and example to her fellow-creatures because of her deep love for the poor, her ministrations to the sick, her unfailing tenderness to her servants, and her sublime conduct towards her enemies. She deserves to be set forth prominently as an inspiration to other generations, especially to the modern age, because while she paraded in the halls of fashion, she attended daily Mass, and devoted herself and her household to the services of the Church. She united a lavish hospitality in the domestic circle with a piety that marked her for greater things in the kingdom of God. She gave her husband every happiness, entertained her many jovial guests in a sumptuous way, while tactfully arranging that Sunday Mass in the parish church should be neglected by no one at her castle. "Who is this woman and we shall praise her? She has done wonderful things in her life." St. Jane Frances de Chantal is such a marvelous and powerful character. An insight into her life and character will awaken all to higher resolves and ideals, and lead the way to spiritual successes that will benefit both the individual and society.

In the picturesque little town of Dijon, in the principality of Burgundy in France, Jane was born on January 23, 1572, the second daughter to M.

Benigne Fremyot, the president of the Burgundian parliament. Both father and mother were of noble blood, and what is more important, splendid types of Catholics. The good mother died while giving birth to the third child, Andre, who became the archbishop of Bourges. Fortunately, Benigne Fremyot was pre-eminently fitted for the care of the three motherless children. He had a keen sense of the necessity of religion in the planting of solid character, and his own example was a constant and efficacious sermon to his children. When Jane was about fifteen, she went to live with her sister Margaret who had just married. Since the two sisters were most devoted to each other, this arrangement was most pleasurable. At the estate of her brother-in-law, Jane found all the enjoyments as well as the dangers that the young could expect in that slippery age. She was careful to preserve herself from the allurements that cause sorrow to many others and cherished the virtues that are dear to Almighty God. Her pleasing disposition along with her attractiveness brought many to seek her in marriage. One in particular appealed to her sister and her husband. This scion of wealth, a Huguenot, concealed his infidelity and feigned Catholicity to win his prize. Jane, however, was not fooled by this pretender. She resisted the efforts of her kin, rejected the worldly advantages which would have moved others. To her sister she presented the truth concerning the suitor's religion and forcibly exclaimed, "I would rather choose imprisonment for life than share the home of a Huguenot. I would rather die a thousand deaths, one after the other, than see myself united in marriage to an enemy of the Church." What an inspiration to others, this firm Catholic stand of the comely Jane! How pregnant with wisdom in days when Pius XI has been obliged to emphasize the will of the Sovereign Master in this matter. Jane, after remaining about five years with her sister, was summoned home by the good father. It seems that the Baron de Chantal had appealed to him for the hand of his child. Both father and daughter realized the excellence from every point of view of this match, and were happy to accede to the request. In 1592, when Jane was twenty years old, the marriage took place.

This union was a success from the start. De Chantal idolized his wife, while she was devotedly attached to one who fulfilled her concept of manhood, who appreciated her ideals, and was ever ready to second her wishes. The baron's estate was at Bourbilly, and there they made their home. Four children, three girls and a boy, blessed their marriage and gave them an opportunity to manifest their thanks to God by an increase in their love of Him and each other. Upon Jane fell the care of the castle and its environs because of the necessity of her husband taking part in the petty wars in which the king was engaged. The property had been neglected since the death of his mother. The young wife shuddered at the responsibility of this vast inheritance but bowed resignedly to the desires of her spouse. In this capacity of manager of the large property of her husband, she demonstrated her fine training and the special tact she possessed as an executive. Everyone was surprised at the marked ability she displayed in handling a very vexatious problem in a most successful way. The tenants had grown careless, the rents had been neglected, the servants had become listless and lazy. Yet Jane, by her marvelous tact, her gentle but firm manner, and her own good example, brought the resources back to where they belonged, and made such marked improvements in the estate, that the baron had reason to congratulate himself on having such a talented spouse.

Her Christian principles of living were at the basis of her conduct of the castle. She ruled by the twin virtues of justice and charity. She saw to it that daily Mass was again celebrated in the chapel of the castle, arranging the hour so that all the servants might be able to be present. This same regard for religion appeared in her relations with those about her for she tried always to respect the rights of others, to be kind and generous with the servants, to afford all an opportunity of enjoying happiness in the midst of their labors. The tenants saw in Madam not one jealous of her rights, anxious to bleed them out of the last penny, but desirous to aid them in the management of their farms, ready to offer helpful advice and eager to share their trials. The sick, in particular, came to appreciate the fine lady the Baron had married. They were her special care. She made it a point to visit each one, to dress them if necessary and to provide them with the best food the castle could offer. Her charity became known all through the countryside so that those who lived within her domains were the envy of their neighbors, and the poor from everywhere were sure of a good meal at the castle from the hands of the baroness herself.

Her entertainment of the many guests of the baron was always a source of admiration; in this she excelled. Nothing was too good for those whom her husband cherished. His friends saw in Jane the perfect wife, docile, affectionate, and hospitable to a fault. Her tact in fulfilling her religious duties at such times never caused any hardship. She arranged everything so that there would be no confusion or conflict. If the house were filled with guests on Sunday, this prudent spouse naïvely suggested that the presence of all the nobility at the parish church would greatly edify the tenants and the servants. In a word, Jane, true to her love for God, so acted that she convinced others of the value of giving first honor to Almighty God.

Such pleasing home-life, such complete union between husband and wife is the foundation of Christian civilization. The charity that was practiced at Bourbilly, the regard for the rights of inferiors, the realization that all are children of the One, Common, Heavenly Father, must be present if society is to flourish, and men to enjoy peace. Where such a spirit presides and prevails, communism will never get a foothold, class-warfare will disappear, and religion will hold its rightful place in the community. What is poignantly needed is the allegiance to God after the manner of this good woman, which wrought such a fine influence upon all who came in contact with her. If all would earnestly attempt to live up to the tenets of religion as she did, what untold blessings would come to individuals and to society. If her sincere love for her neighbor, for the sick, for the poor, were seen in everyone called a Christian, how much consolation would result for the unfortunate!

Into this pleasant atmosphere, this happy home-life, nourished by a loyal husband, a good wife, and four young children, came the grim reaper Death. He sent warning when the baron was visited by a very serious sickness that threatened his life. From this attack that caused such concern and sorrow, he rallied, and was on the road to good health when one day, while on a hunting party, one of his companions allowed his gun to go off, and the bullet entered the Baron de Chantal. The fatal character of the wound was immediately evident. The injured man ordered the priest to be brought, and his wife, who had just given birth to their fourth child, to be notified. Jane surmised the seriousness of the affair and insisted that her place was with her husband. For nine days he lived, bearing patiently his suffering, forgiving his friend, and preparing his soul for God. Jane's grief at his death was insupportable. Her love had been so deep, her devotedness so complete, that it appeared that she would not survive her spouse. Her closest friends feared that her reason would give way. Only the consideration of the four little fatherless children exercised an influence upon the soul that had loved so generously and passionately. Their welfare urged the stricken mother to care for her own health.

The difficulties ahead were greater than anyone imagined. Jane, caring only to live for her children, made a vow of chastity. She pictured either a quiet existence at Bourbilly or a peaceful settlement in the happy surroundings of her dear father who would have been overjoyed at her return with her little ones to make pleasant his declining years. Amid such ideas came word from her vexatious father-in-law that if she did not repair to his castle and make her home there, he would cut off her children from their inheritance. Knowing too well the unpleasant conditions that prevailed at Monthelon, his estate, Jane dreaded the thought of such an existence. Nevertheless, the future of her children ruled out her own peace and comfort. Although she realized clearly the veritable purgatory that would be her lot, although she knew the power that a vixen of a housekeeper exercised over the elder baron, this good woman put aside her own feelings, subdued her rebellious nature, and accepted the harsh sentence of this troublesome father-in-law. Summoning all the courage possible, she prepared to close the castle at Bourbilly where she had spent such happy days with her husband. What tears were shed by the stricken servants and tenants when they saw the

good lady who had cultivated their farms, advised
their children, and cared for them when sick, leaving their environs.

Into the castle of Monthelon she went, determined to place her trust in heaven and to allow
herself to be ruled by the religious principles
which she had so closely followed. The old baron
showed his gruff disposition when Jane tried to
aid him in bettering conditions. The jealous, sus-
picious housekeeper, with her untrained children,
from the outset regarded Jane as an intruder and
possible usurper. Another being than Jane would
have rebelled at the harsh reception that came.
This mother, however, stifling her feelings, over-
looked the disagreeableness of the old baron,
pretended to be unmindful of the suspicions of the
woman, and by patience and charity endeavored
to disarm her associates. With true Christian sen-
timents she treated the five youngsters of the
woman with the same tenderness as her own dear
ones. She kept them clean and tidy, taught them
their prayers and urged all others at the castle to
befriend them. To the impatient baron she was
the soul of kindness. She ministered to his needs,
trained her little ones to be respectful and attentive to him, and meekly blinded herself to his fits
of temper.

Such patient charity, such mildness, was the

result of spiritual motives. Only her deep love for God, her understanding of His Passion, enabled her to be resigned to the harsh, miserable conditions that prevailed at Monthelon. Prayer was the nourishment of this soul amid the vexations of the unruly father-in-law, and the mean innuendoes proceeding from the lips of the woman who controlled him. These trials were opportunities to sanctify her soul, to approach to the Master, to store up for herself "treasures in heaven." Instead of murmuring against the portion that fate had decreed for her, this prudent Christian soul calmly resigned her will to the plans of the unseen but infinitely good God. In this respect what an example she is to many who experience the hardships of life. How consoling it is to see this extraordinarily devout woman thus harassed by persecution. How encouraging to perceive that God blessed her for her spirit of faith, that "He Who readeth the secrets of the heart," rewarded her trust in Him by calling her later to the very heights of sanctity and to the inner courts of His own house. To strive to imitate Jane when in similar circumstances, to practice with her resignation to God, is the best way of assuring for oneself interior peace and the lasting benediction of heaven.

Just as soon as she had the opportunity, Jane

# ST. JANE FRANCES DE CHANTAL

devoted herself to the same religious program that she had arranged at Bourbilly. Mass was had as often as possible at the castle, and she encouraged all to assist thereat. Her own regularity at prayer led to the adoption of similar habits by the children and the servants. She tactfully found a way to minister to the poor and to visit the sick in their homes. Her answer to one who remonstrated with her because of this practice offers a good meditation, "If I did not love the poor, it seems to me that I should no longer love God." How like to St. John the Evangelist, "He that hath the substance of this world, and shall see his brother in need, and shall shut up his bowels from him, how doth the charity of God abide in him?" This Christian conduct by such a noble woman reacted powerfully on those who were forever complaining about the bad habits of the upper class. It gave vigorous impetus to the peasantry to make religion the support of their existence. It made the poor and the sick see the face of Christ compassionating with them in their misery.

Amid these years of patient suffering, Jane had longed in vain for a director who would satisfy her aspirations. When she had gone to Dijon soon after her husband's death, she had a vision of one clothed in a bishop's robe. Not understanding this, she had placed herself under a friar who had

145

been praised by many for his success in helping others. Unfortunately it would seem, he did not understand our Saint's intense spirit. Instead of restraining her desires for mortification, and curbing her readiness to macerate herself, he encouraged this trait. She suffered greatly during these years for want of interior happiness. Providentially her father invited her to Dijon in 1604 to hear the Lenten course to be conducted by the renowned Bishop of Sales. Jane immediately recognized in this holy and prudent Bishop the one manifested by Our Lord for her director. God so arranged matters that Francis recognized the possibilities of the widow and advised her correctly. Jane adopted St. Francis de Sales as her spiritual father and obeyed his counsels to her advantage.

The blessings of a prudent director are seen in the relationship between these souls. The Bishop guided his penitent in the way of simple obedience and gentle charity. He realized that this soul needed to be taught not bodily mortification but mildness and meekness. To her requests that she be permitted to give herself completely to God, he always urged patience. St. Francis de Sales was a director par excellence, "wise to resolve and patient to perform." He offered for mortification greater tact with the children, less harshness with their failings. Her own love for God must not make it difficult for her servants. One of her maids remarked that since her lady had adopted the bishop as confessor, she was holier than ever, but much more considerate to avoid disturbing by her religious practices those under her.

It was in 1610 that this prudent man of God satisfied the desires of his penitent for the religious life. Her three children could now be included in the plan. (Her dear child, Charlotte, had been taken away by death.) Celse Benigne would remain with Jane's father. Marie-Aimee was to marry a brother of the Bishop of Sales. Francoise could accompany her as a pupil. No doubt there were some who criticised Jane for leaving her home and separating her children. That such was, however, the will of God and resulted in His blessing for all concerned is seen not only from the fruits of her action, but also from the actual testimony of her son, Celse Benigne, who some years later freely declared, "I wonder at God's providence in our regard. Had you remained in the world, as we desired, had you taken the care to promote our interests that your maternal love and unparalleled prudence would have inspired, you could not have imagined me better settled than I am. God has given me in my marriage every advantage suited to my rank, age, and disposition."

Francis had evolved an idea that had been agitating him for many years. He felt that there should be a religious institution for women who were widows, and for other earnest souls that could not stand the physical rigors of the existent orders. Jane would be the head of this institute and it would be the means of allowing many devout souls to consecrate themselves entirely to the service of God. Through the tact of the holy Bishop, the President Fremyot acceded to the sincere wish of the baroness. A house was secured at Annecy where Francis de Sales was Bishop from 1602 to 1622. It was a very small and poor place suited to the unpretentious plans of Francis. It was decided to begin the work of God here in order that it might be under the watchful eye of him who had in mind something altogether new in the annals of the Church. The first members of the congregation were St. Jane Frances de Chantal, Charlotte de Brechard, Marie Favre and Ann Cote, a servant. In strict poverty they commenced their novitiate. The foundation was made on Trinity Sunday in 1610. Francis arranged a rule which commenced with Mass at five o'clock. They depended absolutely on contributions from the faithful for their existence. At the beginning this was very trying because their neighbors did not agree with this kind of religious life. Moreover, some of the established convents belittled the strange rule, which, in their mistaken minds, made the way to heaven easier than ever before. These difficulties were no doubt to try the metal of these women. They trusted entirely in the counsels of the holy Bishop and accepted humbly the insults that came from small intellects. They received instructions from him on the essential work of self-conquest, and the way to progress in holiness. Their institute would be consecrated to union with God through charity.

As soon as it was feasible, the Sisters began the visitation of the sick. This was to be their mission. In this way they would fulfill the desires of Christ. Francis de Sales had planned this as their essential active work. They would sanctify themselves through interior prayer and spiritual mortifications and through charity towards their needy neighbors. Jane took up with this desire of St. Francis with the same gentle love that had so impressed the poor at Bourbilly and Monthelon. Her sisters in religion, instructed by this touching example of this noble lady, followed her among the hovels of the unfortunate. The effect on the city at large was immediate; they were captivated

149

by these new religious who were so devoted to those who suffered.

With the establishment of the second convent of the Visitation came an essential change in the nature of the institute. Lyons was the seat of the new foundation. Some Sisters there had tried to live a community-life modelled on that of Annecy, but had failed. They begged Mother Chantal to come and take the house under her protection and guidance. The archbishop gave his consent and St. Francis de Sales encouraged this development. On the feast of the Purification, February 2, 1615, it was canonically erected. When the convent had been established, however, the cardinal-archbishop frowned upon any order of women not being cloistered. This was an innovation which he would not countenance. The good Bishop of Sales had seen the need and opportunity for this departure in the religious life. He was desirous of continuing the patent good that it produced at Annecy. Our saintly head of the Visitation was even more zealous than St. Francis for preserving the external work that was so fruitful. Cardinal de Marquemont, however, was obdurate. The gentle St. Francis at this juncture, although advised by such a learnèd Roman authority as Bellarmine that he could justify his position, accepted the change demanded at Lyons. St. Jane bowed to the decision of her spiritual guide when she was unable to prevail upon him to keep to his original plan for the institute. In 1616, therefore, the rule of cloister was embraced by the Sisters.

This change, in the providence of Almighty God, redounded to the great good of the order, as well as to the advantage of religion in France and even beyond its confines. It would seem that God wanted to manifest in a striking way the value of the humble obedience of St. Francis. St. Jane received requests for institutes from so many cities that she was in a quandary which way to go. In a short time, monasteries were opened at Moulins, Grenoble, Bourges and other places. In each case, there were difficulties to be met. These were seen by the good women as the attempts of the devil to frustrate the kingdom of light. The remarkable result of these new convents upon the indifferent religious life of the laity cannot be passed over. Unfortunately, because of the strength of the Huguenot movement and the worldly spirit that was dominating the better classes, religion was at a very low ebb in France. Providentially, the establishment of the Visitation convents awoke in the hearts of many a realization of the obligations of man to God. Pleasure-minded individuals were stirred in their inner consciences by the heroic sacrifices of these excel-

lent women. Their acceptance of poverty, their
reliance upon the city or town in which they made
their home for the very necessaries of existence,
touched those who paraded their fineries, and insisted upon their creature-comforts. Noble
women, inspired by the example of the first Sisters
of the new institute, considered their own dependence upon God, and abandoned their easy
living in order to give themselves to the service
of the King of Kings. The rank and file of the
laity, due no doubt to the prayers and mortifications of these Sisters in the midst of their city,
came to the sacraments, and brought about a
resurgence in devotion that was in itself a veritable miracle of divine grace. As of old virtue
went out from Christ to heal the woman who
touched Him, so now in Europe in the seventeenth
century, virtue went out from these cloistered
houses of prayer to heal the moral diseases of the
surrounding country. No one observing the evident changes in the religious life of the people
could fail to see that it arose where these monasteries were opened, and that it developed and
spread with their increase and perseverance. The
lines of Shakespeare found their fulfillment in
Jane:

"Those about her
From her shall read the perfect
ways of honor."

God was using this foundation to accomplish a rebirth in the spiritual character of France that made those taking the pulse of the nation exclaim, "Truly the hand of God is here."

These results are an answer to the question sometimes proposed as to what good are institutes of religion that devote themselves only to an interior life. Even some who consider themselves good Catholics shrug their shoulders at the mention of such religious establishments. They, however, are the arsenals whence are made and perfected the bolts that strike the legions of Satan. They are the citadels that protect the country from the ravages of the unseen enemy of civilization. They are the power-houses that radiate throughout the community the supernatural vitality which quickens the dull conscience, which fires the cold hearts and stimulates the bodies that have lost their spiritual force. Such homes of prayer, such institutions of self-immolation, are harbingers of spiritual health to the communities where they abide.

While thus engaged whole-heartedly in the advancement of the kingdom of God, St. Jane did not cease to have a care for her children, and actually had many crosses to bear from this source. Her own dear father died soon after her establishment at Annecy. This grieved her soul much, and caused her to make new arrangements for

Celse Benigne. His later life justified the wise decisions of his mother. Marie-Aimee, happy in her marriage, devoted to her excellent husband, the Baron de Thorens, by sad experience realized the emptiness of this world. The baron, while in the army, was stricken ill, and died very quickly. Marie, about to become a mother, received the shock with Christian resignation. Her child died as soon as born, and the mother, a worthy daughter of St. Chantal, followed her husband and babe, asking only that she be permitted to take the habit of the Visitation and make her religious vows before life departed. Such trials profoundly affected the tender Mother de Chantal, who needed all the strength that religion can offer to endure these tribulations. In 1620 Francoise was married to the Count de Toulongeon who made a fine husband. In 1624, Celse Benigne took Marie de Coulanges to wife much to the joy of his mother who was always worrying about him because of his propensity for duelling. His words, quoted previously, written to his mother are worthy of remembrance. He gave fulsome testimony to the way God had blessed the trust of his mother. To make the cross heavier for Jane, he died in three years, while with the army. Her chief consolation was that he had proved a good child of God, and was fortified in death by the last

# ST. JANE FRANCES DE CHANTAL

sacraments. Five years later Francoise's husband was called by God to his lasting home. Mother de Chantal had now only Francoise and her little children. The widow of Celse Benigne had also died, leaving her only daughter Marie to her father and mother.

Another cross that our Saint felt very poignantly was the loss of her spiritual father, St. Francis. This noble and zealous bishop of God had seen the possibilities for good in the soul of the widow of Baron de Chantal. He had rubbed off the rough edges from her stalwart character. He had been her guide and unfailing support not only for her individual sanctification but also for the great work of establishing and spreading this new religious order. St. Jane had obeyed his every behest, seeing in him God Himself. He, accustomed to the diffident co-operation given to him in many cases when he was on fire for the building of the church of God, was inspired and encouraged by the wholesome, unselfish, mystical spirit of this penitent. It was on December 28, 1622, that Almighty God saw fit to bring to an end the ceaseless labors of this holy man. He had the consolation of offering Holy Mass the very day before his death. Stricken with apoplexy that afternoon, he passed the following evening to enjoy forever the company of Him Whom he had served so devotedly on earth. St. Jane, realizing that the burden of the new order was entirely hers, overwhelmed at the loss of her personal confessor, placed her soul in the Sacred Heart of the Redeemer. Faith comforted her by assuring her that he who had been such a power of strength while in this world, would be more powerful when in the very bosom of God.

To the work of answering the many requests for foundations Jane bent her energies. She was consoled and encouraged by the evident result in the places where the Visitation had been planted. Like the good seed it was bringing forth fruit a hundredfold. Although her strength was sapped by the arduous journeys necessary, by the troubles that the devil always evokes at the prospect of new strongholds of Christ, Mother de Chantal endeavored valiantly to drive her worn body to the limit of endurance for the glory of Her Savior. Her refusal to delay, her insistence on progress was a touching sermon to the Sisters wherever she went, and an inspiration to the Catholic people. What she accomplished in new foundations would be unbelievable if the records did not exist to verify the story. Not only France shared the desire for convents of this cloistered order that was so gentle in its rule while so strict in its interior life, but also Switzerland, Savoy, Piedmont and

## ST. JANE FRANCES DE CHANTAL

Spanish Lorraine had sought and obtained these sanctuaries of virtue and piety. Paris had two convents of the order. Amid all this success, the Saint constantly disclaimed her own responsibility and was ever anxious to be the humblest member of the community. How great was the growth of the order, how much she accomplished, how truly the undertaking was inspired by the Holy Ghost can be judged by the fact that when St. Francis died there were existing thirteen monasteries, when Jane left this earth there were eighty-six.

Like the Savior, on Whom she modelled her life, and to Whom she was so passionately attached, St. Jane experienced in her last years on earth agonies of soul that increased her holiness in the sight of God. What the Master said of St. Paul, "I will show him how great sufferings he must endure for My name's sake." He might have said to St. Jane Frances de Chantal. Interior trials that took the forms of self-mistrust and mental anxiety regarding her own progress in perfection seemed to fasten themselves around her like a serpent. Christ had to suffer alone in Gethsemane and to cry on Calvary, "My God, My God, why hast Thou forsaken Me?" Mother de Chantal walked thus in the path of her Savior. One recalls the words of Francis Thompson:

# HERALDS OF THE KING

"Even so, O Cross! thine is the victory.
Thy roots are fast within our fairest fields;
Brightness may emanate in Heaven from thee,
Here thy dread symbol only shadow yields."

For nine years she had this cross to rid her of the dross of worldly satisfaction, and to unite her more purely to the Heavenly Bridegroom. Higher and higher she went in the esteem of the Sisters who had the good fortune to share the convent of this saint. Her humility, her meekness, her unfailing charity, were an inspiration to her daughters in religion. God manifested His wonderful love for her by giving to those about her an appreciation of her extraordinary sanctity. Wherever she went she was greeted as a Saint. Not only her spiritual children, but also the laity, even the highest nobility, vied to obtain relics of this woman who had done such tremendous things for the purification of religion, and the increase in virtue throughout all France.

The end of her long and fruitful life came on December 13, 1641. She was engaged in the work of the Master when the summons came to report for everlasting honor. The Duchess of Montmorency, whose husband had been put to death by Richelieu, was about to enter the Visitation. During the nine years of her widowhood she had been an example to the world because of her thoroughly Christian life. She had been a constant and generous friend of the Order. Mother de Chantal acceded to the request of this excellent soul that she personally accept her into the monastery at Moulins. This would give the zealous Mother another opportunity to visit some of the convents and to confer with St. Vincent de Paul at Paris for her own spiritual progress and for the welfare of the institute. After her journey to Paris and other places had been accomplished, St. Jane was taken seriously sick at Moulins. To those who mourned this illness she replied that God's will was all that mattered. Generously embracing this last cross, she confided to her religious offspring the good of the institute. Charity alone would be the bond that would link them together. They would honor her most by being perfect religious, keeping away completely the spirit of worldliness, and being guided always by simplicity and charity. Having thus admonished her children, having been fortified by the Sacraments and consoled by the prayers of the Sisters, Jane went forth with hope and love to receive the reward of the faithful servant. Most fittingly it could be said of this noble woman:

"A most unspotted lily shall she pass
To the ground, and all the world shall mourn her."

So persevering was the devotion to her, so enduring was her work (the Order numbered one hundred and sixty-four convents at the time of her canonization), so appreciated was her sanctity, that in 1751 she was beatified, and in 1767 she was pronounced a Saint of God by Pope Clement XIII. Her canonization was the official seal of the Church of God upon the opinion of her contemporaries. As a girl at Dijon she had been an example to those who came in contact with her. As wife and mother she was an ideal for others to copy. As widow at Monthelon she gave forth the pure odor of Christian virtue. As a religious, she graced the earthly courts of God and led others to an understanding of His beneficent ways. How glorious it will be if those who admire her adherence to the teachings of Christ, who are proud of her unflinching, unyielding ideals, who are thrilled by her unflagging zeal in God's service, strive, each in his or her own way, conscientiously and perseveringly, to imitate this Saint in her love for God and neighbor.

# Mother Elizabeth Ann Seton

AN EXCELLENT characterization of one of the ablest American women and one of the noblest Christian souls, Mother Elizabeth Ann Seton, is found in these lines of the poet, William Wordsworth:

"A perfect woman, nobly plann'd
To warn, to comfort and command;
And yet a Spirit still, and bright
With something of an angel-light."

This extraordinary character must always be brought forward when a census of the really great women of all time is being taken. Her name and her fame, as the years roll on, are increasing rather than decreasing. Surely her glory will not perish from the face of the earth. The official court of the Catholic Church has taken cognizance of her holiness and accomplishments, and is inquiring into her claims to sainthood. Her native America paid tributes to her achievements even while she was alive by a homage as wide as the country of the time. For extraordinary fidelity to duty, for exemplification in the highest way of the necessary virtues of Christian motherhood, for sublime and unlimited charity towards the poor and neglected, for intelligent zeal for the training of the young, combined with unusual personal holiness of life, Mother Seton, foundress of the Sisters of Charity, has no superior. Living at the time of the immortal George Washington, she labored untiringly as a true citizen for the formation of character according to the convictions of that genius of statesmanship who declared, "Whatever may be conceded to the influence of refined education on minds of peculiar structure, —reason and experience forbid us to expect that national morality can prevail in exclusion of religious principle." Contemporaneous with that other unique genius, Napoleon Bonaparte, this valiant representative of her sex was sowing in America the seeds of solid virtue, respect and reverence for God and man, while he was tearing down the pillars of civilization and trampling upon the inalienable rights of Creator and creature. To know Elizabeth Seton is to admire and love her. As a fine type of Christian womanhood, as a perfect example of the noblest qualities of the ideal Catholic religious, as a model of beautiful and successful living, she merits the attention of those who are interested in what transcends mere existence.

Elizabeth Bayley was born in New York City, August 28, 1774, the daughter of Dr. Richard

# MOTHER ELIZABETH ANN SETON

Bayley and Catherine Charlton. Both parents
were Episcopalians, the mother's father being one
of the leading ministers of New York. Because of
the early death of Mrs. Bayley, the care of the
child and her two sisters fell to the father, a good
man who was most solicitous for the intellectual
and moral education of his children. Elizabeth
was singularly docile, and manifested as she grew
a deep sense of religion. The Bible had a special
attraction for her; to it she devoted considerable
time. This trait did not interfere in any way with
her social life, which stamped her as a favorite
among the younger set. It might be said of her,

> "Beautiful as sweet,
> And young as beautiful, and soft as young,
> And gay as soft, and innocent as gay!"

When nineteen, she married in the Episcopal
Church of New York, William Magee Seton, son
of a wealthy ship-merchant. Elizabeth displayed
the same fine qualities as wife and mother that
had won for her a coterie of friends as a young
girl. Her home life was wonderfully happy; she
gloried in her five children, three girls and two
boys. With her lovely home, her faithful husband,
and her nursery of children, she was no doubt the
envy of many in the metropolis.

To mar this pleasing picture of domesticity
came the sickness of William Seton. His father

163

had died a few years before, leaving to him in a precarious time, the sole management of the fleet of merchant-ships that was the family fortune. The troubles between England and France made commerce dangerous and unprofitable. The health of the young husband and father, due to the worry from this situation, suffered considerably.

As the one means for recovery, the doctor suggested a voyage to Italy. Seton had been there as a youth and had formed a strong friendship with the Filicchi family at Leghorn, who, as international merchants, were business associates of his late father. The loving wife, undaunted by the quick and sad turn of affairs, anxious only for the welfare of her husband and little ones, was to accompany the patient. She decided to take the oldest child, Anna, with her, and entrust the other four to her devoted sister-in-law, Rebecca Seton. The sea-trip improved William, and their hopes ran high as they neared the shores of Italy. A ghastly blow was to strike them, however, when they reached the port of Leghorn. Because of the news of the yellow fever prevalent in America, the authorities would not allow them to land until they had gone through a period of quarantine. This detention sounded the death-knell of their happy hopes. The quarters destined for them, exposed to the fury of the sea,—"damp, drear, and

bitter cold,"—arrested the progress the patient
had made, and wracked the weak frame beyond
repair. The patient wife, and the obedient child,
Anna, willingly endured the harsh conditions for
the sake of him whom they loved.

The spirit of religion, especially the vivid sense
of the presence of God, was the mainstay of
Elizabeth Seton in this crisis. Without that staff
of strength life would have been insupportable.
The sight of poor Seton daily wasting away, his
moans amid the howling of the piercing winds, her
inability to solace and aid him by any human comforts, and the dangers to her little Anna, were
sufficient to prostrate her. If she had not been able
to murmur with St. Paul, "For I have learned in
whatsoever state I am therewith to be content; I
know how to abound, and how to suffer need; I
can do all things in Him Who strengtheneth me,"
she would have succumbed to despair. In her life
is seen in a wonderfully forceful way the bene-
ficial effect of cultivating a sense of the presence
of God. She was never out of His sight. He was
with her in every time. She could truthfully say:

> "I see His blood upon the rose
> And in the stars the glory of His eyes,
> His body gleams amid eternal snows,
> His tears fall from the skies."

Her Bible, her daily prayers, this constant intercourse with God, were the lights that dispelled the darkness of the quarantine and the sparks that enkindled in the discouraged soul of Seton a supernatural flame which made possible under God a faith in better days in the land to which he was inevitably and swiftly approaching.

To him she imparted her own confidence in God. She showed him tactfully yet wonderfully the love of the Heavenly Father for His children, and the certain and unending reward for those who drink with resignation of the cup of affliction. Whenever he was able to listen, she read to him from the Book of Psalms. Such verses as, "The just shall flourish as the palm tree; he shall grow up like the cedar of Libanus. They that are planted in the house of the Lord shall flourish in the courts of the house of our God," opened up to the sick and dying man a vista of more blessed things that encouraged his soul. The good wife's solid faith, her truly mystical union with God, was a bulwark of strength against the foes that assailed her soul in this dread experience. Every moment not spent in nursing him was given to conversation with her Redeemer. Faith revealed to her in this tribulation the cross of Christ so that she bowed her head in resignation. As a consequence, God, mindful of His promise, never forsook His trusting servant. On her He gener-

ously bestowed graces that enabled her to endure
and become reconciled. What was more, He drew
her closer to Himself, weaning her soul from the
baubles of this world, and unfolding to her a
glimpse of the pearl of great price.

Thus fortified, this valiant woman cared for
her husband and patient both spiritually and physi-
cally until his soul took its leave and his body was
laid away. Worn out by the unbearable conditions
in the quarantine, he lasted only eight days after
his release. On December nineteenth he was gently
transferred to Pisa, where for two days he seemed
to mend. The change for the worse quickly followed. On the second day after Christmas, the
end that meant for William entrance into the
Kingdom of God for which his wife had so well
prepared him, came. With the aid of the Filicchi
family and the Americans dwelling in the city,
Elizabeth laid away the body of him who had
been so devoted a husband.

Without resources, with no one but her little
Anna, the widow of William Seton had to rely on
the good offices of Christian charity tendered by
the two Filicchi brothers, Filippo and Antonio. As
the days went on, she realized how fortunate she
was to have the acquaintance of this family. The
words of the proverb, "A friend in need is a
friend indeed" must have come home to her in her

desolation. They gave to her an example of practical Christianity that spoke volumes. This good Italian family understood what the Savior meant when He said, "By this shall all men know that you are My disciples; if you have love one for another." They had a true grasp of the words of the beloved Evangelist, "He that hath the substance of this world, and shall see his brother in need, and shall shut up his bowels from him; how doth the charity of God abide in him? My little children, let us not love in word, nor in tongue, but in deed, and in truth." The heartbroken widow was received into the Filicchi mansion as a sister. These good Christians lavished hospitality upon the mother and the daughter. Although the Seton fortunes had been completely wiped out by the European wars the two Americans were given every comfort that the minds of the Filicchi could devise. Due to this splendid care, the widow recovered the strength that she had lost in the trying days of the quarantine, and the child Anna once more took on the ruddy health of youth. Little did the kindly Italians realize the great benefit they were doing for the future Church, struggling in America. It was not possible for them to foresee that their Christ-like charity would be the means of aiding countless souls to know and love Almighty God. In their simple way, they sowed the seed that was destined to bring forth fruit a hundredfold.

The religious example of this family was of the best. Faithfully, if unostentatiously, each member of the household fulfilled his or her obligations as a Catholic. Their regularity and devotions at Mass touched the religious soul of this American Episcopalian. The well-conducted ritual of the Catholic Church, with its rich, mystical ceremonial speaking of its reverence for the Body and Blood of Christ, moved her to the depths of her being. She envied them their faith, their serenity, their nearness to the Savior. She sighed to have the Master in Holy Communion. She prayed that she might have the light to know where dwelt the truth. Probably at the beginning, like John Henry Newman, she cried out:

"Oh that thy creed were sound!
For thou dost soothe the heart, thou Church
of Rome,
By thy unwearied watch and varied round
Of service, in thy Savior's holy home."

She was impressed not only by the Church but chiefly by the fidelity of its members to its requirements. She admired and was inspired by lives so consistent with the religious truths professed. She observed with astonishment everybody's exact observance of the rigorous laws of fast and abstinence during the season of Lent. In a word, actions spoke louder than words; this sincere soul was asking herself whether she could do better for God and herself than belong to a church that could do so much for the spiritual welfare of families.

Every good Catholic is thus a power and an advertisement for the religion established by Jesus Christ. This quiet fidelity in the early days of the Church melted the opposition, and brought thousands into the fold of the Master. The same argument is the most convincing one in the present state of society. As the Filicchi were needed to actualize Christianity, so today the world should possess exemplary Catholics in every sphere. Bad example is holding back myriads seeking the solution of life's problems. True Catholicity, as seen in the loyal, obedient sons and daughters of the Church, is a powerful force for the spread of the faith of God.

While every one was so kind to her, Mrs. Seton was anxious to return to her own country and the four children in need of a mother's love. In the milder weather of the late Spring, she prepared to sail. Fortunately for the mother and child, Anthony Filicchi had to go to America to further his business interests. Elizabeth had left her little ones in the affectionate care of her sister-in-law,

Rebecca, verily the other half of her soul. To meet this dear relative was a consolation that the widow was treasuring. What was her consternation and grief on reaching New York to find that Rebecca Seton was on the very threshold of death. She seemed only to await the tender care that Elizabeth would bestow as she slowly wasted to her journey's end. This bereavement in July 1804 was the first of many crosses that the pure and devout soul of Mrs. Seton would experience after her arrival in New York. Destitution would be her portion because of the ruin of her late husband's fortunes. Anguish of mind would encompass her as she tried to provide sustenance for her brood. Her only comfort at this moment was in the thought that she could expect assistance from her many friends as well as from those of her departed William.

Amid these difficulties was the burning, pressing problem of religion. She had made up her mind in Italy that Catholicism was the only choice for true servants of Almighty God. She confided this decision to the Filicchi who gave her what books they had to read and a letter to Bishop Carroll with whom Anthony Filicchi had become acquainted while in the States. With a certain sense of security in her convictions, she decided that it was honorable to reveal her persuasions to Mr.

Hobart, the Episcopalian minister, to whose church she had belonged. By persistent argument, by various pamphlets of the day against Catholicism, he attempted to prevent her taking such a step. Her many friends warned her not to make such a tactical blunder. Fortunately, she happened upon a sermon of the great French pulpit orator, Bourdaloue, while in this quandary. Speaking of the star that guided the Wise Men to Jesus, this brilliant and logical preacher recommended those who were seeking the truth to follow the light God now offered by the representatives of Christ, His priests. This direction was the climax for the sincere Elizabeth Seton. To St. Peter's on Barclay Street she turned her steps on Ash Wednesday in 1805. On March 15, 1805, she made her renunciation of heresy and profession of Catholic faith before Father Mathew O'Brien and Anthony Filicchi. With the peace in her heart that "surpasseth all understanding" she wended her way homeward. She had entered the house of the Lord and He would be her strength in the battles ahead that would try her soul. On the beautiful feast of the Annunciation of the Blessed Virgin Mary she received her first Holy Communion. Under the ægis of God's Mother she would walk when her former friends would not only forsake her but even be her foes.

# MOTHER ELIZABETH ANN SETON

This heroic act of following the dictates of her conscience in the face of the opposition of her dearest friends, is indicative of the exceptional and stalwart character of this staunch convert. She knew the storm that would brew. The sphere in which she moved was hostile to the old religion. The only Catholics in New York at the time were, with a few exceptions, of the laboring class. Catholicism meant for Elizabeth social ostracism. By joining it, she cut herself and her children off from the financial assistance which she would certainly have received among the admirers of her own family and those of the Setons. While visioning all this, she remembered the advice of the Savior, "Seek ye first the kingdom of God and His justice, and all things will be added unto you." Sterling soul that she was, she was sensible of the truth that

> "Once to every man and nation comes the moment to decide,
> In the strife of Truth with Falsehood, for the good or evil side."

If this devotion to her conscience, this acceptance of the manifest will of God, would engender trials, it would also beget unfailing support of Him Who makes the bitter sweet, and rewards even the cup of cold water given in His Name.

The immediate task was to find some means of

income to provide a living for herself and her five children. If it were not for the charity of the Filicchi who gave her about six hundred dollars a year, she would have been destitute. The opening of a school seemed to be the most practical occupation. Success would have crowned this venture were it not for the malicious tongues that asserted that the ultimate purpose was the conversion of the pupils to the Catholic Church. A second attempt, this time as assistant to a Mr. White, also failed because of bigotry. Finally Mrs. Seton took a position as assistant to Mr. Harris, a Protestant. This afforded her a humble existence for three years.

The unfailing providence of God showed itself in the meeting of Elizabeth with Father Dubourg, a member of the Sulpician Order, from Baltimore. This zealous priest saw the devout communicant at early Mass at St. Peter's, and was struck by the spirit of faith evident in her presence. The following day, while she was at the rectory, she was introduced to the visiting priest from Baltimore. He recognized her as the person whose sincerity had attracted him. When he heard of her misfortunes, her perseverance, and her talents as a teacher, he suggested that she go to Baltimore where there was need of a school for the many Catholics there. Elizabeth promised to give the proposition serious attention. When the idea received the sanction of Bishop Carroll and Father Cheverus of Boston, both of whom maintained correspondence with this convert, Mrs. Seton no longer hesitated. Although it was no easy matter to break the ties that bound her to New York, the city of her birth and growth, she was thinking of the souls of her children who needed to be surrounded with Catholic influences and protected against any danger to that faith which was the "pearl of great price." Loving mother that she was, she stifled always her own feelings to further the spiritual and temporal welfare of her little ones. With trust in the bountiful mercy of God, in June of 1808, she bade good-bye to New York and embarked for the episcopal city of Baltimore. Many times during this journey she must have inwardly exclaimed,

> "O Lord! O Love Divine!
>     Once more I follow Thee.
> Let me abide so near Thy side
>     That I Thy face may see.
> I clasp Thy pierced hand,
>     O Thou who diedst for me!
> I'll bear Thy cross through pain and loss,
>     So let me cling to Thee."     (Fr. Ryan)

God gradually unfolded the great designs He had as a reward for the obedience of this convert, and the blessings that were to come through her to the Catholic Church in America. The way was paved with hardships but Elizabeth was a willing and untiring pioneer. One idea ever dominated this simple soul: "I seek not my will, but the will of Him Who sent me." Deeply and genuinely in love with Christ, she was ready to emulate the saints of God to prove her sincerity. In Baltimore, a little house next to the rectory was her first home and school. The good and zealous priests obtained the children who made the venture a success from the start. To increase the happiness of this good woman, there was her opportunity to assist at daily Mass and the other offices of religion. To add to her enthusiasm there was the coming of generous souls asking to share in this apostolate of teaching. This in itself was proof of the blessing and approval of Heaven. It was the wish of that noble father of the Church in the United States, Bishop Carroll, that she who had made the initial sacrifice should be the superior of the organization that was sprouting, and he appeared personally to express his appreciation of this beginning in his diocese, and to invest Elizabeth Seton in the office. Despite her protests of unworthiness, the prudent bishop insisted that she be the superior of the incipient community. Gladly she dedicated herself to the precious work, obediently she responded to the voice of her religious authority, and at his suggestion made simple vows. Her inmost soul is perceived in the declaration she made, "My object in pronouncing them is to embrace poverty, under whose roof I desire to live and die; chastity, so lovable and beautiful that I truly find all my happiness in cultivating it; and, above all, obedience, the sure refuge and safeguard of my soul."

A wonderful impetus was given to the glorious work of Elizabeth Seton by another convert, Samuel Cooper. This man, successful to an extraordinary degree in business, while engaged in travel, saw the necessity also of being wise in spiritual matters. Much prayer and deliberation convinced him that the Catholic Church alone was the haven of truth and the harbor of salvation. He found all that he had expected in the religion of his adoption. Like the young man in the gospel, he learned that one thing yet remained for him; to renounce all he possessed and to follow Christ. He began his studies for the priesthood in St. Mary's Seminary in Baltimore. His money he wanted to devote to Catholic education. Through the mediation of Father Dubourg, he met Mrs. Seton and requested her to use what he could offer for the furtherance of the excellent apostolate she was exercising. Overwhelmed at this new proof of God's unfailing providence, she was happy to accept this gift for her institute. Mr. Cooper had selected a site for the institution he had in mind at Emmitsburg, a village about fifty miles from Baltimore. Thither the school and its teachers would move. There they would have advantages not afforded in the heart of the city. This was the Mount that would take an epochal place in the history of Catholic education in America. Here, under God, thanks to the conscientious daughter of two New York Episcopalians, would develop a religious order that would rival its predecessors in Europe, and would give to the young Church in the United States hosts of devoted intelligent women consecrated by vow to the glory of God and the spread of religion by teaching and every other form of Christian charity.

From many quarters came recruits to form this organization that would receive the official approval of the Church. The first of these volunteers was Cecelia O'Conway, daughter of an exemplary Philadelphia Catholic. There followed Marie Murphy, Ann Butler and Susan Clossy. This was the nucleus that prompted Bishop Carroll to give ecclesiastical recognition to the group, accept the private vows of Elizabeth, and bestow upon her the title of Mother. At her suggestion the congregation was called the "Sisters of St. Joseph."

Due credit must be paid to the priests of the time whose intelligent interest, unflagging zeal, and devoted kindness, inspired, directed, and encouraged Mrs. Seton. Noteworthy among them was the chief shepherd, John Carroll. His fatherly care of his spiritual children embraced every fruitful means of their salvation and sanctification. Though burdened with troubles of every sort, at the request of Antonio Filicchi, he took an interest in Elizabeth soon after she returned from Italy. By his letters he answered the objections of non-Catholics and steeled her soul against the malevolent spirits. He continued this aid amid her trials in New York and gave her a hearty welcome to Baltimore. Father Cheverus of Boston was another whose counsel was of immense support to the new convert. He, with his discerning mind, recognized the superior qualities of this sincere and refined widow. Constantly he wrote to guide her, and prophesied that she would do great things for God. His own life of sacrifice and humility was a powerful influence in forming her Christian character along the lines set forth by our Lord in the beatitudes. Father Matignon of Boston was also a trusted adviser of this extraordinary woman. In Baltimore, the anxious and earnest soul found Father Dubourg a tower of strength. Laboring tirelessly for the conversion of souls, he was glad to devote himself to forming such a helpful ally as Mrs. Seton. These men, along with many others who had entered the ranks of the priesthood, by their repudiation of all creature comforts, by their complete self-immolation, by their charitable interest in every good work, were advertising and spreading the truth in a marvelous degree. Without their interest and co-operation the work of Elizabeth would never have begun, and could never have prospered.

Through such assistance, the religious order, undertaken so simply by the widow Seton with her five children to care for, grew in its interior form and exterior labors. In 1809 it was decided to adopt the constitutions of the Sisters of Charity of St. Vincent de Paul as the community's rule. Bishop Flaget of Bardstown, Kentucky, accepted the office of making such an arrangement with the sisters in France and of begging them to send representatives to Emmitsburg to remain until the new order had obtained the spirit of the rules. The constitutions arrived but the sisters were prevented from sailing by Napoleon. Mother Seton and her council, under the guidance of Bishop Carroll, accepted this set of rules, modifying only what had to be accommodated to American conditions. About the same time, in 1814, Bishop Egan of Philadelphia asked that some of the good religious go to his diocese. An orphan asylum that had been conducted there under the direction of one of the parishes was in a state of collapse because of the difficulty of finding suitable ones to conduct it. Although the proposition was not welcome, since travel was dangerous because of the war with Great Britain and the proximity of British troops, Mother Seton would not refuse the plea of charity. Sister Rose White and two companions undertook this trying mission. In 1817 New York through its bishop, John Connolly, sought the aid of the sisters. Mother Seton cheerfully sent three sisters there to open an orphan asylum. To fulfill worthily these missions, to lay strong foundations for their institute, the spiritual daughters of Mother Seton by diligent prayer, and simple obedience to God, sought the blessing of Heaven.

Let no one imagine that the good Mother Seton had no burdens in this period. The trials and heavy crosses that visited the faithful Elizabeth were many during these years of growth in holiness and zeal in behalf of God's kingdom. Certainly the manifold blessings that sprung from her labors were due in no small part to her patient acceptance of the cup of affliction. Only her strong faith, her profound meditation on the sufferings of Jesus Christ, enabled her to embrace the agony in which she was plunged for so long a time. Each new loss tore at her heartstrings until those about her marvelled at her strength to bear these sorrows. Her noble soul could say to those who sympathized with her:

"The surest way to God
Is up the lonely streams of tears,
That flow when 'bending' 'neath His rod,
And fill the tide of earthly years.
On laughter's billows hearts are tossed,
On waves of tears no heart is lost."

The early deaths of her two dear sisters-in-law, Cecelia and Harriet Seton, were the cause of immeasurable sorrow. Both had followed her into the true Church, Cecelia while Mrs. Seton was in New York, Harriet in Maryland. In the futile hope that Cecelia would regain her rapidly failing health in another climate, she was allowed by her relatives to join Elizabeth at Baltimore. Harriet, devoted nurse, accompanied her sick sister. Charmed by the sweet consolation that the Catholic faith gave to her dear ones, Harriet in 1809, begged admission to their religion. Nobody realized better than she the social loss this step would entail; she was one of the idols of the exclusive New York set. The joy that the three now were having was broken in November by the sudden serious sickness of Harriet. It proved to be a brain fever and carried her off on December twenty-second. That very winter was too severe for the weak lungs of Cecelia. In February she was obliged to keep to her bed. In April 1810 she joined her beloved Harriet. Both of these deaths were severe blows to her who treasured their company, and who was in no small way, a mother to them.

The cup of sorrow was not yet empty. Anna, her oldest and most loved child, was to be taken from her. This daughter had shared all her mother's griefs. She had been her chief aid when she commenced the school at Baltimore. She had shown the tact of a mature woman among the pupils at Emmitsburg. God desired to reward her without the hardships of a long life on earth. For months she patiently bore with the disease that was gradually taking her life. Her only wish was that she might be received into the sisterhood before she passed away. This blessed request was granted to the child who had labored so well to earn it. Her good mother's heart was consumed with anguish as she saw the sufferings that seemed too great to endure. Anna, as a professed member of the institute, died on March 12, 1812. In all these separations Mother Seton bowed her head and tried to say, "Thy will be done." Each new grief was offered in union with Mary Immaculate at the foot of Calvary's Cross, and placed on the altar of God. Each one drew this wholesome character a little further from earth, a little nearer to heaven. Her spirit of obedience to her Father's will, her reliance on His wisdom, her acceptance of His burdens, purified her soul of the dross of this world, and brought down upon her life and her work the precious dew of the love of God.

The cross that Mother Seton had to carry comes into the life of all of God's servants in some form. The old saying is, "no cross, no crown." Christianity is a religion of sacrifice after the example of its Founder Who purchased man's redemption by a life of contradiction and a death of shame. All may not be able to exclaim with that spiritual giant, St. Paul, "I glory in the cross of Christ." All should try to say with the generous Elizabeth Seton, "Thy will be done." These afflictions come from the hand of a Father Who loves us. To refuse them, to rebel against them, is to question His wisdom, and make void the precious graces that follow from them. Mother Seton never complained at the many sorrows that were her portion. She understood that, "To those who love God all things work together unto good." In this she serves as a shining example to all. As God honored her in her bereavements, so He will send

# MOTHER ELIZABETH ANN SETON

His special blessings on all who copy her spirit of Christian resignation.

Although Mother Seton, worn out by these trials, exhausted by her labors for her own children, and for the struggling Church in the United States, felt her health shattered, she was unable to persuade the sisters not to elect her superior for the third time. With her at the helm, peace and contentment reigned among the sisters and passed to the many pupils under their charge. Of her own children, only Catherine and the boys were left to her; the latter were away. Rebecca, the baby of the family, died in 1816. The two boys had received a sound Catholic education, first at Georgetown, then at Mt. St. Mary's College. William had gone to Italy where he served in the house of the Filicchi merchants. He was now at sea with the United States navy. Richard, the younger of the boys, was with the Filicchi now. The community of sisters was flourishing in a way never dreamed of. The vision that Bishop Cheverus had seen in 1809 was a reality. Writing to Mother Seton at that time, he exclaimed, "How admirable is Divine providence! I see already numerous choirs of Virgins following you to the Altar, I see your holy order diffusing itself in the different parts of the United States, spreading everywhere the good odor of Jesus Christ, and teaching by their angelical lives, and pious instructions how to serve God in purity and holiness." The faithful religious urged their mother to lessen her arduous labors that she might be spared to them and the Church for many years to come. Elizabeth Seton, however, had always been a self-immolating follower of her Savior. She had never permitted herself a day's relaxation. On fire with love of God, her zealous soul yearned to exhaust its power in the furtherance of the kingdom of the Master. She would rather wear out than rust out. In 1820 the community saw that their good mother's days were numbered. She seemed to be wasting too rapidly to survive the weakness that was consuming her. Although she rallied and continued to be the inspiration of all, the end was visible. Her only remaining task was to give her religious the example of obedience to the unpleasant cross of physical suffering. This heroic Christian soul understood that:

> "Nothing begins, nothing ends,
> That is not paid with moan,
> For we are born in other's pain,
> And perish in our own."

Guided by the good priests who were edified by her humble resignation and spirit of patience, she accepted her pains as a last opportunity to thank Almighty God for the blessings she had received.

# MOTHER ELIZABETH ANN SETON

She allowed herself only those dispensations from the rule that were ordered by her confessor, the saintly Father Bruté, who was afterwards first bishop of Vincennes, Indiana. On the first day of January in 1821, she received Holy Communion for the last time. Early in the morning of the fourth day of that month, with her sisters and her only living daughter, Catherine, at her bedside, she passed into the company of her long-dead William and her two children that had preceded her, to the kingdom where her sorrows would be over, and her sacrifices would receive their just reward.

The Church in the United States acknowledges the debt of gratitude it owes to this valiant woman. In the face of serious opposition, she obeyed the voice of her conscience and joined the flock of Christ. Persevering amid seemingly insuperable difficulties, she cared for her children and endeavored to be a means of salvation to others. Burning with love for God, she renounced all legitimate worldly aspirations to consecrate herself entirely to her Maker. Obedient to the manifest will of heaven, she became a religious. In that vocation she rivalled the great saints of God in her pursuit of holiness and her enthusiasm for the spiritual welfare of others. Tried by affliction, she embraced it with the faith of St. Paul. At her death she left a well-organized religious congregation to carry on the labors which she had cherished. Though dead these many years, her spirit lives and works not only in her own spiritual daughters, but in the soul of every American Catholic who has come to a knowledge of her life and virtues, and has an appreciation of true genius and sanctity.

# Index

# HERALDS OF THE KING